IMAGINATIONS

MORE THAN YOU THINK

CREATION
HOUSE

JAMES P. GILLS, M.D.

IMAGINATIONS by James P. Gills, M.D.
Published by Creation House
A Charisma Media Company
600 Rinehart Road
Lake Mary, Florida 32746
www.charismamedia.com

Scripture quotations, unless otherwise noted, are from the Holy Bible, New International Version. Copyright © 1973, 1978, 1984, International Bible Society. Used by permission.

Scripture quotations marked NCV are from the Holy Bible, New Century Version. Copyright © 1987, 1988, 1991 by Word Publishing, Dallas, Texas 75039. Used by permission.

Scripture quotations marked THE MESSAGE are from *The Message: The Bible in Contemporary English*, copyright © 1993, 1994, 1995, 1996, 2000, 2001, 2002. Used by permission of NavPress Publishing Group.

Scripture quotations marked NKJV are from the Holy Bible, New King James Version. Copyright © 1979, 1980, 1982, 1992 by Thomas Nelson Inc., Nashville, TN.

Scripture quotations marked KJV are from The King James Version of the Bible.

Cover design by Ededron J. Hernandez

Copyright © 2004 by James P. Gills, M.D.
All rights reserved

Library of Congress Control Number: 2004105942
International Standard Book Number: 978-1-59185-609-2
E-book International Standard Book Number: 978-1-59979-883-7

12 13 14 15 16 — 9 8 7 6 5 4 3
Printed in the United States of America

This book is dedicated to all those who seek to turn their minds and hearts closer to God. May each of us follow in the footsteps of Jonathan Edwards, aligning ourselves with God and finding perfect joy and satisfaction in His thoughts.

Acknowledgments

This book would not have been possible without the contributions and support of many people. First, let me thank my good friend and colleague, Gary Carter. Gary's insight and wisdom have guided countless discussions about how we can focus our minds on Christ and the rich blessings we receive from Him as a result.

I am also deeply grateful to my many staff members at St. Luke's Cataract & Laser Institute who have been partners in prayer and praise throughout the writing of this book. I want to extend a special thanks to Lois Babcock for her support and timely words of encouragement. And to the patients at St. Luke's, let me say thank you for all the examples of faith and focus you have shown.

The contributions of my wife, Heather, have been invaluable. Her love, rooted in the love of God, continues to be a source of inspiration to me.

Contents

Introduction

During the writing of this book, I had a lot on my mind—thoughts I really needed to clean up. My head was a bit "off kilter" because I had been injured, first in a biking accident, then in a skiing accident.

I certainly was able to continue practicing medicine, but I was not able to do the long-distance athletics that had always been such a big part of my life. I could not run or bike or windsurf—all those fun activities I had enjoyed during my after-work hours.

I tried to find other forms of entertainment, but nothing quite filled the bill. My lifestyle and my self-image had changed dramatically, and I was not content.

With so much change in my physical abilities, I decided to go back to something I had done earlier in my life—trading on the stock market. Lo and behold! I made much more money in the market than I did in medicine! Having been trained in the very astute discipline of the psychology of trading, I actually fared better than the managed funds did (with the exception of Internet funds).

However, I became so intense in my trading that it actually started to consume my life. My mind was always filled with the stock market! It was taking time away from my wife, my family, and my friends. More importantly, it was taking away from my time with the Lord.

I became aware of a major difference in my mindset on the days I read the newspaper and neglected the Scriptures. I was not at peace. I did not have deep inner joy. Instead, I was preoccupied with the market and my success. Even though I stood to gain very little personally because most of the profits were designated for charity, the thrill of winning had me hooked! When I realized I was reading the *Investor's Business Daily* newspaper more than I was reading my Bible, I knew I had to get my perspective back.

In the Christian life, some lessons are learned again and again. The lesson brought home to me during this time is that "what we think is what we become."

As I studied the newspaper more and the Bible less, I became weaker in the Word. When we are weak in the Word, our thoughts are open to the assaults of the world—the temptations and lures of sin. And because our thoughts run our life, unless we constantly guard them, we become vulnerable to the powers of sin. Sin robs us of the blessing of God, leading us to poverty of spirit, soul, and body. Consider an ancient proverb that attests to this fact:

> A little sleep, a little slumber, a little folding of the hands to rest—and poverty will come on you like a bandit and scarcity like an armed man.
>
> —PROVERBS 24:33–34

The writer of Proverbs makes it clear that we do not fall into the deep pits of sin overnight—it is a gradual process. We begin that process simply by resting and becoming complacent in our faith journey. We do not guard our thoughts and actions with diligence. Therefore, our thoughts focus increasingly on worldly matters and focus less on godly ones. Those small steps we take toward complacency eventually have huge consequences. It is essential that we constantly guard our thoughts as well as our actions, or we will fall victim to sin.

Thankfully, God wakes us up and intervenes. He shows us where we are stepping out of the path and, as a faithful Shepherd to our soul, brings us back to the cross. He is the living God! He shows us, again and again, that we are saved only through the wonderful, free gift of His grace.

I was challenged by the Word of God. Because I was on crutches for a good part of two years, I could no longer focus on long-distance athletics, as I mentioned. As I filled my head with thoughts of winning on the stock market, it did not take long for me to discover there was no true life there. And I understood anew the impact of my thoughts on my life.

We are foolish when we give ourselves over to the thought patterns of the world and turn our backs on the Lord and His glory! Ungodly thoughts will be followed by ungodly actions that will draw us further away from God.

My prayer, and the purpose of this book, is that each of us will understand how rich our lives are when we focus our thoughts on God. I invite you to explore with me three foundational principles:

- We are what we think; therefore, our thoughts determine our actions.

- Our present thoughts affect how we will spend eternity. When our thoughts are faithfully focused on God, we will be rewarded with an eternal mind-set in this life. We will have a glimpse of the blessings of eternity now, and will be richly rewarded, as well, when we experience His presence in heaven.

- God is most glorified in us when we are most satisfied in Him. Our greatest joy is surrendering our thoughts and our lives to God.

When our thoughts become filled with all the fullness of God we will see His glory, His wonder, His beauty, and His worth in this life. He will be our complete and perfect joy now and for eternity. Amen and Amen!

CHAPTER I

We Are What We Think

Suppose a recording of your thoughts this week was revealed to friends and family and business associates? Would you be appalled or delighted? What would the recording reveal about where your thoughts are based?

To put it another way, let me ask: are our thoughts important? Does it matter what we think? Yes it does, according to the Scriptures:

> Be careful what you think because your thoughts run your life.
>
> —PROVERBS 4:23, NCV

That is the New Century Version translation of Proverbs 4:23, which I think answers those questions quite well. Our thoughts are very important; it does matter what we think. More than that, for each of us, what we think is truly who we are. Whether we are tall or short, rich or poor, black or white, male or female, young or old, our thoughts determine who we are and what we do.

Our thoughts are intertwined with what I call the "imaginations of the mind." Imagination is an ability God has given us that can be used for our good or for our harm. A simple definition of *imagination* is "the image-making faculty of the mind."

These mental images or pictures powerfully influence our thoughts, our ideas, and our attitudes. Imaginations form a pattern of thinking and develop a whole mindset toward life, which determines our creativity, our emotions, our outlook, our self-discipline, our ability to solve problems, and our ability to handle the choices we make every day.

Albert Einstein said, "Imagination is more important than knowledge."[1] That is because all our imaginations affect us, either helping or hurting us. And it is our choice to use them positively or negatively that determines their effect on our lives.

Athletes use their imaginations as part of their training regimen. Olympic runners, for example, create mental pictures of their races before they begin. They imagine all the possible situations that might occur during the race. And they imagine winning.

Most importantly, our imaginations bring us to God as He calls us into relationship with Himself:

> Come to me, all you who are weary and burdened, and I will give you rest. Take my yoke upon you and learn from me, for I am gentle and humble in heart and you will find rest for your souls.
>
> —MATTHEW 11:28

In the Old Testament, two primary Hebrew words are translated as *imaginations: yetser*[2] and *hagah*[3]. Each is used in both a positive and a negative manner, showing the positive and negative power of our imaginations. For example, in the following prayer, *yetser* is used in a positive way:

> O LORD, God of our fathers Abraham, Isaac and Israel, keep this desire [imaginations] in the hearts of your people forever, and keep their hearts loyal to you.
>
> —1 CHRONICLES 29:18

The Hebrew word translated as *desire* (*yetser*) in this verse means *imaginations* and is a part of one of David's beautiful prayers. After King David had dedicated all the materials that the people had given willingly for the temple, he offered a prayer of thanksgiving for God's greatness and glory and power. (See 1 Chronicles 29.) David ended his prayer for the people by asking God to keep this godly imagination—the desire of their hearts—loyal to the Lord always. And he asked that wholehearted devotion be given to his son, Solomon, as well, to obey all the commands of God. On this wonderful day in God's presence, David sought for their minds to be filled with imaginations that were holy and godly.

On a more tragic occasion, God assessed the wickedness of mankind's imaginations, using the same Hebrew word, *yetser*, in a negative sense:

> The LORD saw how great man's wickedness on the earth had become, and that every inclination [imagination] of the thoughts of his heart was only evil all the time.
>
> —GENESIS 6:5

In this verse, *yetser* is translated as *inclination*, and is used to describe the imaginations of man's heart, which were continually evil. It is important to understand that God sent the flood to destroy mankind because of their evil imaginations.

The second Hebrew word, *hagah*, which can be translated as *imagination* (Number 1897 in *The New Strong's Exhaustive Concordance of the Bible*), is used in a positive sense in the following verses:

> But his delight is in the law of the LORD, and on his law he meditates [imagines] day and night.
>
> —PSALM 1:2

> Do not let this Book of the Law depart from your mouth; meditate [imagine] on it day and night, so that you may be careful to do everything written in it.
>
> —JOSHUA 1:8

The Scriptures clearly teach that our meditations—our imaginations—should be filled with the Word of God. These verses stress the fact that all our meditations should be focused on God. It is not an exercise to be taken lightly; it is one that should be done diligently and continually.

Consider the negative use of *hagah* in Scripture:

> Why do the nations conspire and the peoples plot [imagine] in vain? The kings of the earth take their stand and the rulers gather together against the LORD and against his Anointed One.
>
> —PSALM 2:1–2

In this verse, *hagah* is used to describe nations plotting—imagining—how to get rid of God's commands and their responsibility to Him. Their meditations are not focused on the Lord in a positive way. They are full of rebellion, selfishness, and conceit. But, in the end, all their efforts will be in vain. They will not succeed in their evil imaginings. The Lord will always be victorious. And He will guide us into victorious living as well when our thoughts—our imaginations—are headed in the right direction.

In the New Testament, the apostle Paul tells us how we should direct our thoughts:

> Finally, brothers, whatever is true, whatever is noble, whatever is right, whatever is pure, whatever is lovely, whatever is admirable—if anything is excellent or praiseworthy—think about such things.
>
> —PHILIPPIANS 4:8

The true, the noble, the right, the pure, the lovely, the admirable, the excellent, the praiseworthy: these are godly imaginations. When we are filled with these holy imaginations, our actions will honor and glorify God.

Think of it as a clock. Our priorities are the hour hands. They set the general direction of our life. Our thoughts and imaginations are the minute and second hands. They give us our continual energy and our vision.

Our attitudes, our inner imaginations, our inner state of peace or anxiety, determine our actions and words. And our actions and words show what we really are inside. Jesus understood this dynamic when He criticized the Pharisees:

> Woe to you, teachers of the law and Pharisees, you hypocrites! You clean the outside of the cup and dish, but inside they are full of greed and self-indulgence. Blind Pharisee! First clean the inside of the cup and dish, and then the outside also will be clean.
>
> —MATTHEW 23:25–26

The inside of the cup, our mind-set, is what is important. It is simply a fact that our imaginations determine our actions. Jesus says it bluntly:

> For out of the heart come evil thoughts[4] [imaginations], murder, adultery, sexual immorality, theft, false testimony, slander.
>
> —MATTHEW 15:19

We will fall, we will fail, if we let the wrong thoughts direct our actions. We must open our minds and hearts to the true imaginations of life—God and His eternal promises revealed to us in His Word.

Most importantly, our fate for eternity hangs in the balance of what we are thinking today. Our thought patterns for this life will mold our lives for eternity. We will be rewarded for our faithfulness when we keep our thoughts focused on Him.

What God really wants is for our inner lives to be directed toward Him! He does not care for outward display or "shows"— what we wear, our skin color, our appearance, our height, our bank balance. He cares about our thoughts and how they direct our actions, both now and for eternity.

The foundation of life—for all the details of life, and for all of life's endeavors—is that we are focused on Him and that our thoughts remain faithful to Him now and, consequently, for eternity. The secret to daily life is to turn all of our thoughts to Him so that the priority of our imagination is to always think of Him.

Searching for Satisfaction

Let's go back to that recording of your thoughts we discussed in the previous chapter. What were you thinking about? Were you thinking about whether or not you have what you want—enough money, enough success, enough time? Were you thinking about whether or not you are happy? Do you feel fulfilled or do you feel that "something is missing" in your life?

These kinds of questions were first initiated at the beginning of humanity. The first created couple, Adam and Eve, had everything they could ever want in the Garden of Eden. Yet they wanted more. And Satan knew how to use that imagination—that desire for wanting more—to lure them away from focusing on God first. Though God had clearly communicated one prohibition to Adam regarding eating from the tree of the knowledge of good and evil, on penalty of death, Satan challenged God's command and His motive for giving it:

> "You will not surely die," the serpent said to the woman. "For God knows that when you eat of it your eyes will be opened, and you will be like God, knowing good and evil."
>
> —Genesis 3:4–5

Choosing to believe the Serpent's deception, first Eve, and then Adam, ate the fruit. The result? Death to their wonderful relationship with God, their Creator. They were banished from the Garden of Eden, where everything had been given to them, and sent to work the land for themselves. The seeds for each of our struggles for choosing between God and worldly desires were sown with the actions of Adam and Eve.

I know people, and I am sure you do also, who are always dissatisfied with their lives and are desperately searching for satisfaction. Some imagine they will find satisfaction in their work, so they go from job to job, never finding the perfect fit. Others think satisfaction is found in what they can get out of a relationship with another person. So these folks drift from relationship to relationship, unable to give of themselves and never receiving very much from others. Still others settle for fleeting sensual pleasures rather than lasting satisfaction. They end up abusing alcohol or drugs. Some see life as a series of meaningless sexual encounters. While others desire so much of what others have that they steal, or even kill, to get what they want.

Why do people waste their lives in these meaningless and destructive pursuits? The analyst Sigmund Freud spent a lot of years observing human thought and behavior, struggling to find answers for this human dilemma. He concluded that it is just our nature. No matter what we have, it is never enough. People cannot be satisfied because they are selfish; they always want more. Freud thought our condition was hopeless.

But that's not what God thinks!

God has created all of us with the strong desire for true contentment. We all have a void in our hearts that yearns to be filled. We may seek all kinds of activities and relationships to find satisfaction. But God knows that nothing the world offers will ever satisfy us. According to worldly standards, we will never have enough money, enough fame, enough success, or enough love.

That is why God intervened so powerfully in a way that has changed my life and can change your life! He sent His Son, Jesus Christ, to die on a cross and rise from the dead. He let His Son die so that we could live. He sent His Son as a sacrifice for sin that had separated mankind from Him since Adam and Eve disobeyed His command. Christ went to Calvary so you and I could have eternal life—a relationship with God that fills the void in our hearts now and for eternity. He made right the relationship that Adam and Eve had broken. Consider the beautiful way the apostle Paul describes God's remedy for our sin:

> Very rarely will anyone die for a righteous man, though for a good man someone might possibly dare to die. But God demonstrates his own love for us in this: While we were still sinners, Christ died for us.
>
> —ROMANS 5:7–8

Now, Sigmund Freud didn't understand this kind of love. It doesn't make sense to the natural mind that someone would give up his life for another. But, in Jesus' teaching, He took normal human perspectives and attitudes and turned them upside down. He tells us that what the world offers us—money, jobs, activities, relationships—is not the prerequisite for our satisfaction. Jesus offers the true priority of life that will give us total satisfaction—focusing on our spiritual relationship with Christ as opposed to the natural "pleasures" of life. The apostle Paul understood this spiritual principle for finding satisfaction when he wrote:

> The man without the Spirit does not accept the things that come from the Spirit of God, for they are foolishness to him, and he cannot understand them, because they are spiritually discerned. The spiritual man makes judgments about all things, but he himself is not subject to man's judgment: 'For who has known the mind of the Lord that he may instruct him?' But we have the mind of Christ.
>
> —1 CORINTHIANS 2:14–16

Discovering true satisfaction in Christ will never make sense to those focused on worldly desires. Our wonderful union with the mind of Christ will appear foolish to the world. But it doesn't matter. When we have surrendered to the pure and perfect love of Jesus Christ, our imaginations will be centered on Christ!

"I have come that they may have life, and that they may
have it more abundantly."
—JOHN 10:10, NKJV

As we accept the eternal life offered by Christ, each of us can
know, deep in our soul, how powerful it is to have our thoughts
and imaginations filled with, engulfed in, and focused on the living God. We can attest to the new life that comes from faith in
Christ flowing through us, enveloping us, guiding us, and healing
us. We are united with Christ. He lives in us!

Freud and Christ are at opposite ends of the spectrum of imaginations—total *selfishness* and total *satisfaction*—respectively.

Total selfishness is insatiable desire. It reflects more than normal desires and a healthy lifestyle. It is characterized by total
uneasiness and unrest. It manifests as neurosis, by which one
can still function in society, but not well. And, ultimately, it is
psychosis, in which people are no longer able to function accept-
ably—they steal, abuse verbally or physically, and kill. Selfishness
is a cascade of inordinate desires that are never satisfied.

Total satisfaction for the human heart can only be found in
relationship with Jesus Christ. Our "wants" are never filled until
they are filled by Christ. God created us for this purpose—to find
our full satisfaction in Him. Author John Piper says it this way:
"God is most glorified in us when we are most satisfied in Him."[1]
We find true contentment when we believe the promises of God
and accept the eternal life He has given us through Jesus Christ.

The search for satisfaction is innate to our human condition.
Many people seek satisfaction through imaginations that are not
of God. They have imaginations of worldly power, sex, money,
popularity, and success.

But we can only be truly and completely satisfied through
Jesus Christ! God gives us perfect joy and peace when we choose
to think about Him and fill our minds with godly thoughts. Jesus
confirmed this fact to His disciples:

As the Father has loved me, so have I loved you. Now remain in my love. If you obey my commands you will remain in my love, just as I have obeyed my Father's commands and remain in his love. I have told you this so that my joy may be in you and that your joy may be complete.

—JOHN 15:9–11

There is a story about an unhappy king who sent for the court magician to ask how he could find contentment. The magician said the king needed to find the shirt of a man who was truly content and to wear that shirt day and night for a month.

So the king sent his men to search throughout the kingdom to find such a man. It took months before they finally returned. They reported to the king that they had found only one man who was content. The king stormed around and demanded, "Well, where's the shirt? Don't keep me waiting!"

The men paused and then said, "The man who was truly content had no shirt."

Contentment can never be found in the abundance of possessions, in success, in a career, or in physical achievements. The king who looked for contentment had everything except contentment because he was looking for it in the wrong places. Contentment never comes from external sources. It can only be found through setting our minds—our imagination—on knowing Christ, who will meet all our needs.

Psalm 23:1 says, "The LORD is my shepherd, I shall not be in want." God is our portion; He will provide for us. All we need is to choose to be near Him and walk with Him. That imagination, that faith in Jesus Christ, has changed my life! Hear how this dynamic changed the apostle Paul:

> ... I have learned to be content whatever the circumstances. I know what it is to be in need, and I know what it is to have plenty. I have learned the secret of being content in any and every situation, whether well fed or hungry, whether living in plenty or in want. I can

do everything through him who gives me strength.

—PHILIPPIANS 4:11–13

The apostle Paul wrote this while he was sitting in a Roman prison. He did not know how long he would be there. He didn't even know whether he would survive or be put to death.

But it didn't matter because Paul had discovered the key to true contentment: he knew this Jesus who had died on the cross for him. He knew this Jesus who rose from the dead for him. He knew this Savior who walked with him every day through the power of the Holy Spirit. He knew this Jesus who had given him a home in heaven!

Paul had faith in God's eternal promise that He would provide for him all that he needed in life. Paul knew, in his head and in his heart, that God would give him strength to meet all his needs. And he could rejoice, regardless of his external circumstances, because he had faith in God's provision, not just for a moment, but for all eternity. That faith-filled imagination is what gave the apostle Paul God's perfect peace and satisfaction.

Jesus not only did that for Paul; He provides that satisfaction for you and for me! We can walk with Him; we can talk with Him; we can feel His presence every day—now and for eternity—if we choose to meditate on our relationship with Him continually.

This godly imagination gives us a totally new perspective for life and satisfaction. Money, fame, and success do not matter. We don't want, and we certainly don't need, what this world offers in order to enjoy heart satisfaction. Those temporal desires are no longer important. We see what's truly important—a personal relationship with God through Jesus Christ that begins now and lasts for all of eternity!

Sadly, we live in a world filled with evil imaginations and earthly philosophies. We're barraged with a constant flow of worldly concepts through television, radio, newspapers, magazines, books, and the Internet.

That is why the words of Paul are so important. They remind

us that we can be content knowing that we have eternal life! What can Madison Avenue advertising offer to compete with a relationship with Jesus Christ? We no longer have the mind of the world, so we are no longer lured away by the lying promises of the world's imaginations that try to ensnare us.

Genuine contentment in life is found only in the deep, permanent, and beautiful mind-set of Christ Jesus. Actions guided by His wisdom, with faith in His promises, produce that sense of satisfaction, as Scripture declares:

> Because your love is better than life, my lips will glorify you....My soul will be satisfied as with the richest of foods; with singing lips my mouth will praise you.
>
> —PSALM 63:3, 5

This God-centered attitude can change your life! When you learn to find satisfaction in the eternal promises of God you will be filled with peace and joy, patience and thanksgiving. No longer a victim of selfishness, you will be satisfied with God's eternal provision.

Worry and fear are gone! Bitterness and anger have been replaced with forgiveness and love. We are confident that He will provide for each of us now and for eternity according to His promises:

> Come, all you who are thirsty, come to the waters; and you who have no money, come, buy and eat! Come, buy wine and milk without money and without cost. Why spend money on what is not bread, and your labor on what does not satisfy? Listen, listen to me, and eat what is good, and your soul will delight in the richest of fare.
>
> —ISAIAH 55:1–2

This is a tremendous Gospel—Good News—offer. Come to the Lord. Let Him provide. Here is the energetic call of the Almighty God welcoming the dissatisfied heart to come to Him to find true satisfaction.

According to the Scriptures, only in God's free grace can we find satisfaction. Otherwise, we labor for that which does not satisfy us. Often, we are concerned with outward appearances and are absorbed with our own importance and the impressions we make on others. We are consumed with the physical life rather than the inner life. And we exhaust ourselves searching for external satisfaction. Sometimes we get so focused on the details of daily life that we lose sight of the overall picture. May the words of Paul encourage us:

> Therefore we do not lose heart. Though outwardly we are wasting away, yet inwardly we are being renewed day by day. For our light and momentary troubles are achieving for us an eternal glory that far outweighs them all. So we fix our eyes not on that is seen, but on what is unseen. For what is seen is temporary, but what is unseen is eternal.
> —2 CORINTHIANS 4:16–18

The world tells us material goods and measures of success are important. The Bible tells us that what is really important are the eternal priorities of God. What we can see is temporary; it doesn't last. We need to put our hope in the invisible and the eternal promises of God.

Focusing on our eternal relationship with Him changes our daily behavior. Earthly measures of success are not important because we are in an eternal relationship with Him. With an eternal perspective, we realize we don't need to be successful in other people's eyes. We don't need to try to live up to their expectations.

We have everything and become everything that satisfies—in Christ! The possessions we have mean nothing. We do not need to worry and fret about matters that are not important. Our momentary afflictions are nothing compared to the eternal joy and eternal glory we're going to receive in Christ Jesus.

Most importantly, we are being transformed! The Greek word that describes this transformation of mind, and then of life, is *metanoia.*[2] *Meta* means change; *noia* means thoughts. As a noun, *metonia* means change of mind, repentance. According to the Scriptures, our thoughts are being changed as we focus on God:

> Do not conform any longer to the pattern of this world, but be transformed by the renewing of your mind. Then you will be able to test and approve what God's will is— his good, pleasing and perfect will.
>
> —ROMANS 12:2

> But we all, with open face beholding as in a glass the glory of the Lord, are changed into the same image from glory to glory, even as by the Spirit of the Lord.
>
> —2 CORINTHIANS 3:18, KJV

God transforms our thoughts—our imaginations—as we focus on Him. A basic concept of salvation is having a God-centered attitude. In *metanoia,* we see how God's grace wipes away our old ways of thinking, our old imaginations. We see what is truly important. We are His children, and we are engulfed in His love.

We cannot be the same after we have had this transformation— this *metanoia.* Our thoughts and actions are different because we are anchored in our relationship with God. We are satisfied with Him and Him alone. Let's examine the words of Paul again:

> I have learned to be content whatever the circumstances. I know what it is to be in need, and I know what it is to have plenty. I have learned the secret of being content in any and every situation, whether well fed or hungry, whether living in plenty or in want. I can do everything through him who gives me strength.
>
> —PHILIPPIANS 4:11–13

Knowing how to be content when we are in want requires an extra measure of diligence. All of us struggle at times with wanting more or with comparing what we have with others. Remember the secret that Paul shares with us. We can do everything through Christ. We do not have to possess more than we have now or possess more than other people. We need nothing more to satisfy us than our imaginations of Christ, having our minds filled with His thoughts.

It is just as important that we stay focused on Christ when we are "well-fed" as when we are in need. Being content when we are prosperous means we are still content in God's provision for our lives. And we give God the glory for what He has provided. Neither do we become proud of having so much, because we know God has given it to us; we do not claim to have achieved it by ourselves.

We must remember that He is all we should want and, in an active sense, He is all we do want. He will always satisfy us! He will always fill us! He is all-sufficient, now and for eternity! In this way, we can grow in our satisfaction in Jesus Christ and become faithful followers through His grace. We become intimate with Jesus; we commit our lives to Him; we seek to let His mind and His thoughts be ours.

Why is growing in Christ so important? Because our thoughts today affect our future and shape who we will be for eternity! Remember: you are what you think!

Imaginations focused on Christ allow us to feel God's presence in all circumstances. They allow us to reach up and see eternity! These godly meditations allow us to see God's vision of life for us, because our hearts are melted together with the heart of God in eternity.

We need to imagine ourselves eternally with God. We need to imagine the Holy Spirit always with us. We need to incline our heart toward Him. When we come to the Lord, we are content in Him. We find satisfaction because we know what we have right now is sufficient because of His generous gift. We need to seek nothing else.

Living in faith means learning to be satisfied with our relationship with the Lord through Jesus Christ. We are not distracted by the world when we are satisfied in His promises. When our minds are fixed on Him, we are weaned away from our earthly focus and are faithfully and fervently focused on Christ, our love for Him, and our commitment to Him.

As we seek this blessed transformation, let us turn our eyes, our hearts, and our minds to Jesus and the transforming power of His death and glorious resurrection. We find perfect peace and joy when we are engulfed in our Creator, Redeemer, and Sustainer, the one who liberates us from the selfishness that leads to sin and death. In God, through Christ Jesus, we find eternal satisfaction, eternal love, and eternal life. Let me encourage you to turn your mind from lesser pursuits to seek complete satisfaction in Him!

CHAPTER 3

Fixing Our Eyes on Jesus

A life filled with satisfied imaginations is glorious! Those imaginations allow us to be captivated with God. We want to embrace God. We know, in our heads and in our hearts, that His promises to us are real. These faith-filled imaginations bring us a genuine sense of satisfaction and joy in the life God has given us.

But what happens when worldly thoughts sneak in? Do they really affect our lives—and our actions?

Yes, they do. Remember, our thoughts direct our actions. We are what we think. If we think selfishly, we are not satisfied with Christ. We are not filled with imaginations of an eternal relationship with Him. Our daily thoughts affect our lives for eternity.

The test for whether the imaginations of our daily lives will help us or hurt us is simple: do they reflect the mind of Christ? Paul emphasizes in his letter to the Philippians that the foundation for a peaceful, joyful, godly life is godly thinking. Let's look again at his instruction:

> Finally, brothers, whatever is true, whatever is noble, whatever is right, whatever is pure, whatever is lovely, whatever is admirable—if anything is excellent or praiseworthy—think about such things.
> —PHILIPPIANS 4:8

The best way to get rid of a bad habit is to replace it with a good one. The basis of replacing selfish imaginations is Jesus Christ.

Struggles with the lures of this world are displaced in our

minds as we think on our Lord Jesus Christ. He will help us guide our imaginations.

Then we will wake up in the morning full of thanksgiving, joy, and love. Our hearts will be upright in rejoicing, rather than beaten down in cynicism, and will become conquerors for God, not conquered by the world. For that reason, the Scriptures declare:

> Let us fix our eyes on Jesus, the author and perfecter of our faith, who for the joy set before him endured the cross, scorning its shame, and sat down at the right hand of the throne of God. Consider him who endured such opposition from sinful men, so that you will not grow weary and lose heart.
> —HEBREWS 12:2–3

The person of Jesus Christ should always be before us and incorporated within us. We need to make sure we think of Jesus and start out the day with Him, and then be conscious of Him throughout the day.

A story about Mother Teresa illustrates this point. A group of people had been with her for a while and asked what they could pray about for her. She replied that they might pray that she never got so involved in Jesus' work that she forgot Jesus. She wanted to make sure that she was thinking first of Jesus in whatever she did. She didn't want the zeal for her work to replace her zeal for Christ.

Now we all have thoughts and desires. The outcome, though, depends on whether we are satisfied in God's promises or whether we covet the material goods and other temporal "blessings" of this world. We will either live in a confining jail of the mind or we will live a life engulfed with God.

When we're satisfied, our thoughts are focused on God. We're filled with faith, peace, and love because we know He is providing all we need.

At the other end of the spectrum is a life of sin dictated by insatiable want. All the sin in life stems from failing to believe God will provide. I would like to call it the "psychosis of wanting." We are selfish creatures who will destroy ourselves and those around us because we do not have faith in the promises of God. Lacking self-control, we pursue our inordinate desires, seeking satisfaction apart from God. The Word of God clearly states that if we do not control our thoughts, they will destroy us:

> Like a city whose walls are broken down is a man who lacks self-control.
> —PROVERBS 25:28

We need to control our thoughts or they will destroy us. For example, there is a difference between sexual desire and lust. Desire is normal and healthy. It leads to the sharing of love with one's spouse. It enables us to have children. It lets us be male or female. But lust is desire gone awry. It's a focus on the world that goes beyond what God says is good and right for us. Uncontrolled desire can destroy us.

The unchecked desire, or lust, for any of the things of this world isolates us from God and will destroy us. These "vain imaginations" can include our occupation, possessions, social status, love of sports, sensual interests, or anything else that can fill our minds and become an obsession. We are so easily fooled by the wrong things. We need to have Jesus before us at all times. He promises an escape from the destruction of uncontrolled desire:

> No temptation has seized you except what is common to man. And God is faithful; he will not let you be tempted beyond what you can bear. But when you are tempted, he will also provide a way out so that you can stand up under it.
> —1 CORINTHIANS 10:13

There are no new or original temptations. God has seen them all. He has seen many people in the same struggles we face every day. And God loves us so much and so faithfully that He will provide an escape for us in those moments of greatest weakness. He will throw us the lifeline, but it is up to us to grab it.

We do not have the strength within ourselves alone to overcome temptation. That is why we are instructed in Ephesians 6:10 to "be strong in the Lord and in his mighty power."

We cannot change our thoughts by our own power. The only power we have is to choose to submit and surrender to God. Through His sovereignty and power, then, we are able to overcome the imaginations of the world, the evil that comes from Satan, and the sin that comes from unbelief. We need to accept the Lord, find our strength in Him, and then we will overcome.

How do we respond to the constant battle between our faith in God's promises and our desire for worldly possessions and worldly acceptance? We need to return to God's Word to remember His promises to us. The psalmist considered God to be his only worthwhile treasure:

> Whom have I in heaven but you? And earth has nothing
> I desire besides you.
>
> —PSALM 73:25

Do we desire what the world offers or, rather, the rich blessings of God? Every day we must choose whether we focus on a personal relationship with Jesus Christ or on temporal pursuits. Every day we must decide whether we are going to be directed toward the Lord or toward Satan. It is important that we have a constant desire to be renewed in our imagination day by day. Then we can get rid of the bondage that inhibits our lives and get rid of the thoughts we know are wrong.

We react to the events of each day, not because of a set of codes or rules, but because of a personal relationship with Christ. This dynamic of life is not a strange enigma or mystery; it is an absolute truth of focus. When we re-pattern our thought processes to be Christlike, we will have the joy of a Christ-filled life.

CHAPTER 4

Faith in Action

We know we are supposed to focus our thoughts on Jesus. But how does this apply to our daily lives? Jesus tells us to imagine building a house:

> Therefore everyone who hears these words of mine and puts them into practice is like a wise man who built his house on the rock. The rain came down, the streams rose, and the winds blew and beat against that house; yet it did not fall, because it had its foundation on the rock.
> —MATTHEW 7:24–25

What happens if we do not put God's words into practice? Jesus warns us of the consequences:

> But everyone who hears these words of mine and does not put them into practice is like a foolish man who built his house on sand. The rain came down, the streams rose, and the winds blew and beat against that house, and it fell with a great crash.
> —MATTHEW 7:26–27

Focusing our thoughts and then letting godly actions spring from those thoughts is the essence of a fulfilled life. Our thoughts and actions must be aligned. We cannot think one way and act another or we will end up torn apart. But when our thoughts and actions work together, our faith and experience turn hope into God's manifest reality. And our worldly desires are destroyed!

This is an important step to take as believers. When our

thoughts and actions work together we can see evidence of our growing spiritual maturity. God wants us to grow. He has bestowed His gifts to us for this purpose:

> To prepare God's people for works of service, so that the body of Christ may be built up until we all reach unity in the faith and in the knowledge of the Son of God and become mature, attaining to the whole measure of the fullness of Christ.
>
> —EPHESIANS 4:12–13

A faith is mature when we experience the fullness of Christ. Our desire to be filled with His fullness increases daily as we grow to see God's glory, His wonder, His beauty, and His worth. When we mature, our thoughts and actions spring forth from the fullness of Christ, and we allow Him to be our joy and our portion. Our imaginations are integrated with Him.

Therefore, we must mature spiritually just as we mature physically and emotionally. In order to mature physically, we need nutrition and conditioning. Maturing spiritually is no different. Spiritual nutrition comes from the Word of God. Spiritual conditioning comes from aligning our thoughts and actions with His will.

> Anyone who lives on milk, being still an infant, is not acquainted with the teaching about righteousness. But solid food is for the mature, who by constant use have trained themselves to distinguish good from evil. Therefore let us leave the elementary teachings about Christ and go on to maturity....
>
> —HEBREWS 5:13–6:1

How do we know that we are maturing in Christ? Hear the warning written by James:

> Do not merely listen to the word, and so deceive yourselves. Do what it says.
>
> —JAMES 1:22

James tells us we must act out our faith or our faith is without maturity. We are mature when our house is built on the foundation of the Word and our actions flow from that foundation.

We also need to examine the motives behind our actions. Are our actions guided by Christ or by selfish desires? The apostle Peter exhorts us to right motivation:

> If anyone serves, he should do it with the strength God provides, so that in all things God may be praised through Jesus Christ.
>
> —1 PETER 4:11

Our actions must be guided by God through the Holy Spirit. Imagine a cup in a bucket of water. The cup is not only filled with water, it is surrounded by water. That is a picture of how the Spirit should direct us—the Holy Spirit filling us and surrounding us.

Let me tell you a story about a man who wanted to design a boat. He didn't want to build the *Titanic*, mind you, just a simple sailboat. Yet he wanted this sailboat to be one of the prettiest in the world. So he set to work on his dream. He did everything possible to make beautiful the parts of the boat that were above the water—the part of the boat that people could see. But underneath, he cut corners. When the engineer suggested that a certain amount of weight be applied to the very lowest part of the keel, he ignored the advice. "Oh, no one will see that part of the boat" he reasoned. So he used less weight to cut his costs.

Finally the day came to put the boat into the water. He brought all of his friends out to the pier to watch the launching of his boat. Everyone was awed at the boat's majestic appearance. But when the boat began to sail away from shore, a heavy wind capsized it.

This boat owner chose to see the world in one way—giving priority to the external, visible appearance. His internal focus was misdirected.

As Christians, it is essential that we have the right focus. We cannot merely act with the visible behavior appropriate for a Christian. We need to be guided in our actions by our foundation of faith and confidence in God's eternal promises:

> For it is we who are the circumcision, we who worship by the Spirit of God, who glory in Christ Jesus, and who put no confidence in the flesh.
>
> —PHILIPPIANS 3:3

Paul is warning his readers about putting too much stock in good works and external symbols of faith, such as circumcision. He says the followers of Christ are the "circumcision," and that circumcision is a rendering of the heart to focus their lives in worship of the Lord (Romans 2:29). They rejoice in Jesus alone. They have no confidence in rules and outward actions. Their confidence is rooted in the promises of God.

> So do not throw away your confidence; it will be richly rewarded. You need to persevere so that when you have done the will of God, you will receive what he has promised.
>
> —HEBREWS 10:35–36

God has promised that He will provide for us now and for eternity. When we are totally in love with Christ and are faithfully focused on Him, we will be blessed with riches beyond our wildest imaginations! Therefore, it is essential that each of us has a circumcision of the heart, cutting away selfish ambition and being filled with God's Spirit (Romans 2:29). Then our actions flow from His will and we mature spiritually.

What are your imaginations? Is your thinking based on what is above the water line, or what is below? Actions based on external priorities reveal a lack of Christian growth. Remember, only the internal spiritual realities—your relationship with God—live forever!

CHAPTER 5

Anticipating Eternity

Thoughts and actions united in purpose with the Spirit of God reveal our spiritual growth as Christians. When we mature in our faith, we experience the fullness of God, which is a joy beyond description. Our ability to grow in Christ is limited only by our ability to focus our thoughts on God and our choosing to be faithful to Him.

Besides the need to grow in our faith, there is another reason we should focus our thoughts on God and walk faithfully with Him. There is a direct connection between this present life and eternity. How we focus our minds now will determine our eternity.

For example, those who develop their musical capacity appreciate the varieties and intricacies of classical music. They have a deepened capacity and appreciation. Those who have not developed this capacity hear music but do not experience as much beauty when listening to the same melodic patterns.

In that same way, some have suggested that believers who have developed a deeper capacity for God on earth will have a deeper joy and glory and wonder in heaven. What God bestows on us in heaven is related to the spiritual capacities we develop in this life. The way we live now is the way we anticipate eternity.

God will preserve our mind-set and our personality for eternity to the degree that we have become like Christ. He saves us by His grace, and He is going to preserve us, who were made by His Word, for eternity.

In response to His grace, we are commanded to be faithful in our imaginations so we can constantly focus on Him:

So ther., men ought to regard us as servants of Christ and as those entrusted with the secret things of God. Now it is required that those who have been given a trust must prove faithful.
—1 CORINTHIANS 4:1–2

God's Word tells us we will be rewarded for being faithful, in thoughts and actions, to His Word and His promises.

Whatever you do, work at it with all your heart, as working for the Lord, not for men, since you know that you will receive an inheritance from the Lord as a reward.
—COLOSSIANS 3:23–24

God rewards each of us for being faithful to Him in our thoughts and actions. Faithfulness is not merely external. It is not just how faithful we seem in our actions—going to church, donating time or money. Our secret thoughts need to be faithful to Him as well. Through our faithfulness in thought and action, we are thankful, we are surrendered, and we are abandoned to Him. Our faithfulness to Him determines our eternal reward.

For the Son of Man is going to come in his Father's glory with his angels, and then he will reward each person according to what he has done.
—MATTHEW 16:27

We will be evaluated for how faithful we have been. Not only will we be rewarded, we will also face judgment.

Do not be deceived: God cannot be mocked. A man reaps what he sows. The one who sows to please his sinful nature, from that nature will reap destruction; the one who sows to please the Spirit, from the Spirit will reap eternal life.
—GALATIANS 6:7–8

If we want eternal rewards, we must be diligent in all our desires of Him. We must keep our thoughts faithfully focused on Him and let our thoughts guide our actions. Remember, we are what we think and we will be rewarded accordingly:

> For we must all appear before the judgment seat of Christ, that each one may receive what is due him for the things done while in the body, whether good or bad.
> —2 CORINTHIANS 5:10

Paul issues a call to us: our actions must reflect thoughts focused on Christ, because we will be held accountable in eternity. Paul is not saying that we are saved by our good works. We are saved solely by grace. But he reminds us that if we say we are followers of Christ, we must live as followers of Christ. Then we can appear before Christ at the time of judgment with joy in our hearts. This is the reason for our diligent focus on Him. Hear this promise:

> And without faith it is impossible to please God, because anyone who comes to him must believe that he exists and that he rewards those who earnestly seek him.
> —HEBREWS 11:6

Our faithfulness in keeping our mind focused on Christ will be rewarded in eternity. We must be faithful to Christ and never grow weary of imagining Him first.

May each of us choose to earnestly seek the mind of Christ, letting our thoughts of Him guide our actions and our lives. May we be diligent in all our desires for relationship with Him—now and for all eternity!

CHAPTER 6

Changed Hearts, Changed Lives

Is it enough to know about God? Is it enough to see Christ as an important historical figure? How does our knowledge of God relate to our life?

The great theologian, John Wesley, struggled with these questions. In his early adult years, Wesley faithfully served as a priest in England and the United States. He committed himself to Bible study, prayer, fasting, and serving others. He acknowledged that Jesus is the Son of God. But, according to his own testimony, during this time he studied only with his mind. He did not understand in his heart that the promises of God were true for meeting his every need.

Then, at age thirty-five, he was transformed! During a meeting with fellow Christians in Aldersgate Street in London, Wesley had a deeply personal encounter with faith. While Martin Luther's preface to the commentary on the Book of Romans was being read, Wesley became electrified. He later called this spiritual awakening a "quickening" in his soul. He said, "My heart was strangely warmed."[1]

No longer were his beliefs merely intellectual. His mind was made new. In this Aldersgate experience, he realized the promises of God were true for him, and he developed a passionate relationship with the Lord. Wesley went from being a dead theologian to a living Christian. He was turned upside down by realizing that what he knew in his head applied to his whole being. What he knew transformed how he lived!

It is a life-changing experience to be touched by God. It changed John Wesley. It has changed me. It can change you. God welcomes each of us. He wants each of us to seek Him and to focus our hearts and minds on Him. Then we can feel the presence of God awakening within us. He reaches us with His infinite love. He touches us with His wisdom, knowledge, and discernment. Our hearts are inclined to Him.

We are made new when we open our minds to the promises of God. He will touch us and transform us. The Scriptures confirm this reality:

> I will give you a new heart and put a new spirit in you;
> I will remove from you your heart of stone and give you
> a heart of flesh. And I will put my Spirit in you and move
> you to follow my decrees and be careful to keep my laws.
> —EZEKIEL 36:26–27

What an awesome experience to have our hearts changed by God! The active force of God's love is a critical agent of change. He heals us and freely bestows His love on us. He gives each of us a new heart, a heart that loves Him and loves to follow Him. Our imaginations are filled with Him.

Not only that, we now have His Spirit within us, guiding us, comforting us, supporting us, and encouraging us. From the time we commit ourselves to God, we hear Him and know His presence through the Holy Spirit. Walking under the power of the Holy Spirit, we are obedient to His commands.

When God quickens us and transforms our faith, we are totally different. We have experienced *metanoia*. We do not try to improve or change our old ways of thinking and acting. The old ways are demolished! We are completely new!

> And we, who with unveiled faces all reflect the Lord's
> glory, are being transformed into his likeness with ever-
> increasing glory, which comes from the Lord, who is
> the Spirit.
> —2 CORINTHIANS 3:18

When we embrace Christ as Lord and Savior, we put ourselves into God's hands. We let Him work through us to be transformed. We begin to reflect His glory. And as we are transformed, we experience greater and greater glory.

We have a new mind, a new hope, a new life! We are new beings in Christ. We are filled with His love, His perfections, His perfect strength, His past grace, His present grace, His future grace. The apostle Paul describes these "glorious riches":

> I pray that out of his glorious riches he may strengthen you with power through his Spirit in your inner being, so that Christ may dwell in your hearts through faith. And I pray that you, being rooted and established in love…may be filled to the measure of all the fullness of God.
> —EPHESIANS 3:16–17, 19

Paul explains how Christ dwells in our hearts by faith. God dips into His infinite riches and pours them into our hearts, strengthening our inner thoughts with His Spirit. And that faith is rooted and grounded in His love for us.

These verses also explain our ultimate goal in life—to be filled with the fullness of God. Our goal of transformation, and our heartfelt longing, is to be filled with all the fullness of God.

Henry Brandt talks about the distinction between being *transformed* or being merely *reformed*. We try to reform ourselves by ourselves: physically by exercising, intellectually by pursuing higher learning in a college or university, spiritually by going to church. This attempt at personal reformation is also an attitude we project toward others. For instance, I know a lot of people who have struggled to "reform" their spouse.

We cannot be transformed as followers of Christ by ourselves. Our minds can never do it alone. It is only through the love and grace of God that we are transformed.

Transformation comes from the Spirit of God living within us, activating us. He ignites a spirit of peace that comes from our total commitment—a spirit of *shalom*! *Shalom*, a Hebrew word for peace, is more than just a warm, fuzzy feeling. It is God working within us to create eternal peace and satisfaction in Him, through the guidance of the Holy Spirit.

Does that change who we are? Absolutely and completely! Even our countenances reflect this dramatic change:

> Those who look to him are radiant.
>
> —PSALM 34:5

We will radiate Jesus Christ and what we have been given— His grace, His love, His mercy, His joy, His forgiveness—now and for eternity. We are finally made complete, not in ourselves, but through Christ.

There have been moments in my life when I have been participating in a worship service, for example, or enjoying God's world during my running exercise, and a special awareness of Christ comes over me. It is a feeling I cannot describe with words. But I am fully aware of God touching my heart in a deeply personal, transforming way during those moments.

When we are transformed, our imaginations of God are not just an intellectual exercise. We have a passion for Him—not just intellectual knowledge, but an inner desire so that He affects all of our being.

This quickening experience makes us truly imagine God as our Creator, Redeemer, and Sustainer. We see God as the one who gives us all blessings. And we understand that His love is the only love that can satisfy our hearts. His forgiveness is the greatest acceptance we need. His wisdom is the greatest guide we have; therefore, we submit to His perfect will. We see God's love overflowing into His grace, His grace into His mercy, His mercy into forgiveness for our sins—now and for eternity. This is the faith that transforms us!

Consider the lives of two of Jesus' disciples who sinned against Him. The first man, Judas, went to the Jewish authorities and plotted the betrayal of Christ. The second, Peter, after Jesus' arrest, when he was confronted about his relationship with Jesus, denied knowing Christ. Both despaired of their acts, but only one sought repentance.

Judas confessed his sin. "I have sinned," he said, "for I have betrayed innocent blood" (Matthew 27:4). But he didn't take the next step of faith, which is to seek God's mercy and forgiveness. Instead, he went away and hanged himself. Peter, on the other hand, went back to the other disciples. In their company he discovered the empty tomb and the risen Lord. He rejoiced, but also knew he would be called to account for his actions.

After His resurrection, Jesus asked Peter three times, "Do you love me?" (John 21:15–17). Three times, Peter answered, "Yes." And all three times, Jesus gave Peter a critical role for the budding church: "Feed my sheep." Jesus, the good shepherd, entrusted the flock to a man who had denied knowing Him.

Peter had a transforming faith in Jesus Christ that was missing in Judas. Judas calculated his every move and intentionally rejected the Lord. Judas might have known, intellectually, that Jesus was Lord, but he did not imagine a personal relationship with the living Lord. Peter walked with Jesus differently. He had a transforming faith based on his personal relationship with Jesus. In a moment of fear, Peter rejected Jesus. But he later repented of his actions. His moment of doubt was erased by his life of faith.

Peter found his satisfaction in the person of Jesus Christ, and he could imagine the Lord's forgiving arms wrapped around him. He knew he had eternity stretching ahead of him with Jesus. And Jesus not only restored him, but gave him a place of great honor and responsibility.

A personal relationship built on transforming faith will make the difference in our lives today. We can live, we can float, we can dwell, we can rest, we can be interwound with, we can be engulfed in the God of creation who made Himself known and visible in the person of Jesus Christ. The psalmist asked for this divine life:

> Satisfy us in the morning with your unfailing love, that
> we may sing for joy and be glad all our days.
>
> —PSALM 90:14

This psalm was written by Moses about the Israelites wandering in the wilderness. They had refused to believe God and go into the Promised Land. Moses prayed that the new generation would learn to find God as their true satisfaction.

How does this search for satisfaction relate to us? On our own, we will never grasp this full measure of satisfaction. Our imaginations are too feeble. We will only be transformed when we are activated by faith, when we live full of faith that His promises are real for our lives. Then we will have true satisfaction, contentment, and joy!

CHAPTER 7

Amazing Grace

If God asked you why He should let you into heaven, what would your answer be? Your good deeds outweigh your bad? You are a member of such-and-such a church? You practice the golden rule? You try to keep the Ten Commandments? Those are not adequate answers according to the Scriptures:

> For it is by grace you have been saved, through faith—
> and this not from yourselves, it is the gift of God—not
> by works, so that no one can boast.
>   —EPHESIANS 2:8-9

Jesus' encounter with a rich man reveals these faulty attitudes of righteousness. (See Matthew 19:16–20.) This rich young ruler came to Jesus and asked Him, "Teacher, what good thing must I do to get eternal life?" (v. 16). Jesus told him to keep the commandments: "Do not murder, do not commit adultery, do not steal, do not give false testimony, honor your father and mother, and love your neighbor as yourself" (v. 18).

The young man said he had done all that, but wondered what was still missing. He asked Jesus, "What do I still lack?" (v. 20). Jesus saw that the man's thinking was in error. A person cannot earn eternal life by performing good works, by keeping the rules and the law. Jesus' response opened the man's eyes to his failure:

> Jesus answered, "If you want to be perfect, go sell your
> possessions and give to the poor, and you will have

> treasure in heaven. Then come, follow me."
> —MATTHEW 19:21

Jesus offers gracious hope to any who seek Him. All we must do is follow Him. Sadly, the man chose to not follow Christ.

> When the young man heard this, he went away sad, because he had great wealth.
> —MATTHEW 19:22

The disciples, who had heard the whole conversation, were confused. They asked Jesus, "Who then can be saved?" (v. 25). Jesus reminded them of God's love and grace and power:

> With man this is impossible, but with God all things are possible.
> —MATTHEW 19:26

Jesus makes it clear that salvation is never won by human attainment. Instead, salvation is available only by God's grace, when we accept Christ's atoning sacrifice. Faith is the gangplank to walking into God's grace.

Yet we keep trying to change God's rules. Our image of God is distorted. We can imagine that we have to work for our salvation—that we have to earn it through our deeds and our thoughts, rather than accepting His grace and trusting in His sovereignty. By sovereignty we mean that God is in charge, in control, and working all things for our good. In short, God is God and is acting as God. We can imagine that we have to give up all of life and become a stoic or ascetic. We can imagine that we have to live by many rules and be legalistic in our approach to others.

Remember, we cannot show the Lord that we are worthy of salvation by anything we do. All we show by our works is that we are imperfect people with faults, failings, and false imaginations. We will never earn a position in eternity based on this faulty thinking.

None of us can meet the demands of God's law. None of us can earn His salvation by our obedience. We can fool ourselves and become perfectionists, as the Pharisees were. We can focus on what we should do, but still lack the love that makes His grace a reality in our lives.

God did it all for us. Christ died on the cross so we would be freed from sin. As He hung on the cross, Christ declared: "It is finished" (John. 19:30), and we must receive His finished work to have forgiveness for our sins. That overwhelming act of love saves us. His generous sacrifice for our sins keeps us from despair that we will never earn a place in heaven. It is only the work of Christ on the cross that saves us. Salvation is God's gift to us. And we do not need to despair thinking that He cannot redeem us. Nothing is too difficult for God.

If we imagine that we must prove ourselves to God (and in a similar way, that we have to prove ourselves to others), then surely we will be miserable, ill-at-ease, and never finding peace. Eventually, we will get tired of trying to prove ourselves and be tempted to totally turn away from God. The imaginations of legalism lead to an empty heart that does not find satisfaction, fulfillment, or redemption. Those faulty imaginations ultimately lead to self-destruction.

We are not transformed by our own strength, but by faith in God's power to save us. We can envision faith activating God's grace and salvation. It is only by God's healing grace and forgiveness that we are made clean. We live in His grace. We find eternity in His grace. We find His presence in His grace. Listen to the apostle Paul:

> Remember that at that time you were separate from Christ, excluded from citizenship in Israel and foreigners to the covenants of the promise, without hope and without God in the world. But now in Christ Jesus you who once were far away have been brought near through the blood of Christ.
>
> —Ephesians 2:12–13

The blood of Christ has the power to cleanse us of all the world's thoughts and actions. The blood of Christ has the power to transform us! Let us come to the Anointed One, the Messiah who mediates between God and man. We need to focus our thoughts solely on Christ. When we see Him as the essential element of our being, godly thoughts and actions will follow.

It is only through God's grace that He loves us enough to touch us and restore us, wretched and sinful as we all are. We all have failings. We all have sins. God's grace cleanses us, washing away our past, which is filled with failures and mistakes. God's grace upholds us today, as we struggle to let our imaginations focus on Him and leave worldly thoughts behind. His grace will provide for us tomorrow and for eternity. We have His grace forever!

When God restores our hearts through His grace, we are deeply and intimately bound to Him. We begin the journey toward a life that is more abundant, peaceful, and joyful. We focus our minds and hearts on the one who saves us, redeems us, and transforms us. Praise be to God for His matchless grace! Amen!

Chapter 8

A New Perspective

What do you think happens to us when we die? Do you think about death's approach? Do you keep busy in your daily life with work and family and activities to keep from thinking about death, living in denial of its reality? Do you believe heaven is real, but irrelevant? I know a lot of people do not like to think about death and what will happen to them. But all of us have an appointment with death. There is no way to hide from it.

The Bible tells me that I will spend eternity with God through my relationship with Jesus Christ. Therefore, death to this life is just a graduation to heaven. In fact, I am already living just a bit of that eternal life here on earth. And because He loves me that much, He will take care of me every day. This is the power that transforms my imaginations! The apostle Paul had that kind of transforming faith. It allowed him to write these words while in prison, not knowing whether he would be executed or allowed to live:

> For to me, to live is Christ and to die is gain....I am torn between the two: I desire to depart and be with Christ, which is better by far.
>
> —Philippians 1:21,23

Paul understood that heaven is real. More than that, to him it had deep relevance to the way he lived his life here on earth. Heaven is more than anything this world has to offer—more than life itself! Heaven is eternity in the presence of the living God. Paul could live in anticipation of his future in heaven.

How do you imagine eternity? Here is one image I like to use. Our Father owns the land on both sides of the river. The side we are on now is the life we live in this world. The other side of the river is eternity. In this image, I can see myself eternally cared for by Him on both sides of the river. My image of eternity is positive, not negative. It allows me to be strong and courageous when facing death. It has comforted me as well when fellow believers have died.

God has promised to keep us in His presence. That is why we can look at death without fear. That imagination is what allowed Paul to write these words:

> Where, O death, is your victory? Where, O death, is your sting?...But thanks be to God! He gives us the victory through our Lord Jesus Christ.
> —1 CORINTHIANS 15:55, 57

Christ's resurrection from the dead frees us from our sins and frees us from death. The prison doors that locked us in worldly thinking are shattered! We have the eternal bliss of being engulfed with Him. What an imagination of the heart!

John Bunyan described this divine relationship so beautifully in his book, *The Pilgrim's Progress*. Bunyan told the story of Christian, the pilgrim whose only goal was the Celestial City—eternity with God. Christian encountered trials and temptations along the way and found loyal companions who encouraged him. Finally, he saw the city, glorious to behold. But before he could enter the gate, he had to cross a turbulent river, and there was no bridge.

He understood that the River Jordan is the River of Death. It is a treacherous crossing. Christian entered the river and the waves crashed over his head. He was turned upside down. He cried out, afraid he would die and never reach the city. And he found strength in his faith that God would provide. Then he recalled the promise God made to the people of Israel through Isaiah:

When you pass through the waters, I will be with you;
and when you pass through the rivers, they will not
sweep over you.

—Isaiah 43:2

Once Christian's faith was firmly established, the river became shallow, and he easily finished his crossing. His faith led to peace. And that peace directed him toward God, wanting to touch the Lord in the Celestial City. He went through the gate and entered the paradise of God.

Through Jesus, death is swallowed up forever! Death is conquered eternally. Death is no longer a barrier between us and God, but is a doorway to Him. When we step into heaven, we will say, "This is my God! I've waited for Him. I rejoice in Him." As the prophet Isaiah wrote:

In that day they will say, "Surely this is our God; we trusted
in him, and he saved us. This is the Lord, we trusted in
him; let us rejoice and be glad in his salvation."

—Isaiah 25:9

We know Him now, and we look forward to that day of seeing Him face-to-face in heaven. Everything else is trivial. We will be with Him for eternity! We have eternal victory through Christ!

I have a friend whose body is dying. Yet he is full of peace and knows he will be engulfed with God for eternity. The light of the Celestial City, of heaven, allows him to imagine eternity. That vision keeps him going, even through cancer treatments and as he faces death.

Eternity is where we put all our hopes, our goals, our cares, and our concerns. Where there is Christ, there is hope. Where there is Christ, there is joy. I have seen this joy in fellow believers who were dying. They weren't afraid. They weren't worried. They were actually ecstatic toward the time of their death. They knew, they had seen, Christ's hands carrying them toward an eternity of perfect peace and joy! They understood, with the apostle Paul:

> If we live, we live to the Lord; and if we die, we die to the
> Lord. So, whether we live or die, we belong to the Lord.
>   —ROMANS 14:8

What a promise! We belong to the Lord! We have eternity with Him! For me, believing these eternal truths makes life more exciting. Getting up in the morning and going to bed at night, eating my daily meals and going through my daily activities—all are richer experiences.

This eternal perspective becomes the focus for our lives, the foundation for our lives. We no longer see ourselves like we once did. We now live in anticipation of His eternal presence. We make all of our decisions based on that premise. We see that life on earth is short and soon passes away. But we are with the eternal God forever!

Can we follow the example of John Wesley? When he was quickened by the Holy Spirit, he gained a new way of looking at the world. He saw eternity with Christ—an eternal relationship, an eternal feast with his Lord and Savior. He could say with the prophet, Isaiah:

> On this mountain the Lord Almighty will prepare a feast
> of rich food for all peoples, a banquet of aged wine—the
> best of meats and the finest of wines. On this mountain
> he will destroy the shroud that enfolds all peoples, the
> sheet that covers all nations; he will swallow up death
> forever. The Sovereign LORD will wipe away the tears
> from all faces; he will remove the disgrace of his people
> from all the earth. The LORD has spoken.
>   —ISAIAH 25:6–8

These verses are rich with the themes that help us imagine the Lord. Isaiah is telling us about the presence of Jesus on earth and His death and resurrection. Through Him, we have seats at the table of the richest, most exquisite feast—a feast greater than physical food and drink. It is a feast in which God is our portion. And we are at this feast for eternity.

This eternal reality contradicts the consumer culture in which we live. We are barraged by media messages telling us to live for today, to get as much as we can, as quickly as we can. We are told to measure our success by dollar signs and to compare ourselves with those around us. The apostle Paul warned the young man, Timothy:

> But you, man of God, flee from all this, and pursue righteousness, godliness, faith, love, endurance and gentleness. Fight the good fight of the faith. Take hold of the eternal life to which you were called when you made your good confession in the presence of many witnesses.
> —1 Timothy 6:11–12

When we focus on eternal imaginations, we can understand better how little the possessions and measures of worldly success matter. We can point ourselves toward eternity with Him and we can work enough to be satisfied in our daily lives without being consumed by the cares of the present day. Instead, we are consumed by our focus on our future with Him—a future that begins now as we are engulfed in His presence:

> But one thing I do: Forgetting what is behind and straining toward what is ahead, I press on toward the goal to win the prize for which God has called me heavenward in Christ Jesus.
> —Philippians 3:13–14

The prize for which we run is not ours; it is Christ's prize. The Lord wants our minds in union with His mind now, so we can live in eternity with Him, fully engulfed in His presence. The true prize is our eternal relationship with God through the person of Jesus Christ.

The hustle and bustle of everyday life sometimes makes it easy to forget eternity, but eternity must be the backdrop for every part of our temporary life on this planet. George Gilder said, "Men lust, but they do not know what for. They wander, and lose track of the goal. They fight and compete, but they forget the prize. They spread seed, but spurn the seasons of growth. They chase power and glory, but miss the meaning of life." [1]

Hear the words of Jesus:

> "Do not store up for yourselves treasures on earth, where moth and rust destroy, and where thieves break in and steal. But store up for yourselves treasures in heaven, where moth and rust do not destroy, and where thieves do not break in and steal. For where your treasure is, there your heart will be also."
>
> —MATTHEW 6:19–21

Remember that rich young ruler who couldn't give up his worldly possessions to follow Christ? The love for the material goods of this world kept him from following Christ. Is it the same with us? Do we trust God to provide treasures in heaven? Can we give up the material goods of this world? Jesus asks all of us to prefer heavenly treasures to all the wealth and riches this world offers.

When we open our arms to embrace Christ, our love for the possessions of this world fall away. We cannot selfishly cling to them if we are reaching out to Christ now and for eternity. Because we have that eternal imagination in our minds, we have a new outlook in our daily lives. We have a new satisfaction and contentment. We have genuine peace.

I have seen people in difficult life situations that would seem unbearable. Yet their satisfaction in the Lord, through their transforming faith in His eternal provision, supports them and guides them. Their imaginations are centered on the Lord and on His desire that we find our greatest delight in Him. Their actions reflect the spiritual wisdom that flows from faith in God's promises. They have a genuine sense of satisfaction, and they are filled with hope, peace, and joy. They have grasped the eternal vision of God for their purpose in life.

When we are filled with God's eternal perspective, we concentrate on the inner workings of the heart and mind-set, with its imaginations and attitudes. When we see more clearly how we fit into God's eternal plans, we live looking forward to eternal fellowship with God. Author John Piper refers to God's "future grace"—where we are engulfed with His presence forever and alive with Him forever.[1]

In essence, God says to each of us, "Come up here and be with Me; come up here and be My child; come up here and be like the Savior, and be in My presence forever." May each of us join God in the eternal feast of His blessings— both now and forever!

CHAPTER 9

The Motivation Equation

Let's imagine ourselves having received now and for eternity every blessing God has for us—His love, His mercy, His grace, His forgiveness, His joy. Do we let those things motivate our lives day by day? Or does something else motivate us? More money, more power, more comforts, more recognition, more leisure time, or more sexual relationships? If love for God is not our motivation, then sin will be. The apostle Paul lists specifically sinful motivations:

> The acts of the sinful nature are obvious: sexual immorality, impurity and debauchery; idolatry and witchcraft; hatred, discord, jealousy, fits of rage, selfish ambition, dissensions, factions and envy; drunkenness, orgies, and the like.
>
> —GALATIANS 5:19–21

Paul describes in those verses four categories of worldly, or vain, imaginations:

- Sensuality: sexual immorality, impurity, debauchery, orgies

The sensual realm can be quite normal when enjoyed according to biblical principles. But when sensuality strays from a godly focus, it becomes abnormal. It can destroy us.

- Sorcery: idolatry and witchcraft

Sorcery includes worship of all kinds of things that are not of God. Any worship is abnormal and sinful when it is not focused on the true God.

- Substance: drunkenness

Substance abuse is very common. Substances can be food, drink, tobacco, or any substance that takes over our spirits, taking us away from God.

- Social sin: hatred, discord, jealousy, fits of rage, selfish ambition, dissensions, factions, envy

Social sin is the strife that takes over when we lose our love for God and for others.

These four "s" motivations stem from a fifth "s": selfishness. Remember that total selfishness is the opposite of total satisfaction. Do we have an eternal perspective or are we filled with worldly thoughts? Worldly thoughts stem from selfish motives—a focus on our own desires, rather than focusing on God's eternal grace and provision. We think we can rely solely on ourselves. No longer do we find our satisfaction in God's promises. Instead, we isolate ourselves from Him, thereby planting the seed for additional trials and temptations.

My good friend, Dr. William Standish Reed, president of Christian Medical Foundation International, says there are two systems that shape us: clinging to the dust and clinging to God. When we cling to the dust we are holding on to earthly appetites. We have the values of this world—the desire for material goods, material symbols of worldly success. When we cling to God, we have a new heavenly appetite for the Word of God and the eternal kingdom of heaven.

"Healing, blessing and wholeness, creativity, godly love, joy unspeakable, and a magnificent inward spiritual rejoicing are the products of the spiritual life rather than of the natural life," says Dr. Reed.[1]

If we want the transforming power of Christ in our lives, we must reject the self-centered thinking that the world promotes. We must keep an eternal perspective. That means we must be willing to totally change our way of thinking. We must be willing to do away with our worldly thoughts and surrender to Him.

We are filled with lasting imaginations of peace, joy, thanksgiving, hope, and love when we focus on Jesus Christ. We don't just think about Him in passing as we go about our daily routines. When we are transformed by faith, we must let His thoughts be our thoughts, His mind-set become our mind-set, His imaginations be our imaginations. We surrender our selfishness to seek complete satisfaction in Him, as the apostle Paul taught:

> Your attitude should be the same as that of Christ Jesus: who, being in very nature God, did not consider equality with God something to be grasped, but made himself nothing, taking the very nature of a servant, being made in human likeness. And being found in appearance as a man, he humbled himself and became obedient to death—even death on a cross! Therefore God exalted him to the highest place and gave him the name that is above every name, that at the name of Jesus every knee should bow, in heaven and on earth and under the earth, and every tongue confess that Jesus Christ is Lord, to the glory of God the Father.
> —PHILIPPIANS 2:5–11

Our minds are changed, our imaginations are changed, so that we imagine Jesus, we think Jesus, and we live Jesus. We change the filter of our minds, no longer looking back through a filter of worldly desires and selfishness. Instead, we see through the filter of Christ's mind. The apostle James tells us how this is possible:

> Submit yourselves, then, to God. Resist the devil, and he
> will flee from you.
>
> —JAMES 4:7

Christianity is the opposite of selfishness. We must be completely unselfish to hand over our lives to Him. We must surrender to Him our hearts, our minds, our wills, our sense of independence, and pride. "Self" must be placed on the cross where we imagine our earthly thoughts, our worldly imaginations, dying with Christ on that cross. Jesus taught us to die to self and live in Him:

> If anyone would come after me, he must deny himself
> and take up his cross and follow me. For whoever wants
> to save his life will lose it, but whoever loses his life for
> me will find it.
>
> —MATTHEW 16:24–25

Death to self is essential if we are to surrender to Him. Death to self destroys the false imaginations that tell us our own frail, feeble human powers are sufficient to provide for us. We refuse to accept the vain imaginations, restless thoughts, and worries of this world. When we abandon ourselves to Christ, we walk in joy and love as the children of God.

When our imaginations are focused on Christ, we see the world in a different way. Our motivation is no longer to achieve earthly status and success. We are motivated by the gorgeous beauty of being with the Lord for eternity. We see eternity reaching out before us.

Surrendering to Him means we are putting our roots down in the love and mercy of the Lord. We must live with the images of surrender to God and then act on those images. We no longer have a sinful mind, but we have the mind of Christ. We must think and act like God to truly enjoy being His children.

Surrender makes us more reflective so that we seek His will and unite our minds with His. We do not give up our thought processes as mindless children who follow with blind obedience. Rather, we take the simple truth of His grace and think it through, so that science, knowledge of God, and God Himself all merge together in a meaningful relationship. With a simple, yet strong, faith we have a reflective, informed understanding of the mind of God as it is revealed to us in the Bible.

The more we let Him nurture us and guide us, the greater our transformation will be. We receive His love, His grace, His forgiveness, and His strength as we align our minds and our thoughts with Him. The fruit we produce—our actions—stems from the thoughts focused on Him. We must apply His mind in our daily lives and let our actions and works flow out of our state of praise and worship to God.

What we own in life is not important. What owns us is very important. Do our desires for worldly success own us? Or have we truly surrendered ourselves to Him? Taking on the mind-set of Jesus, surrendering to His will, transforms our priorities. When we take on Jesus in our person, we see life differently. We see it through the heart and mind of Jesus. We do not merely include Him as part of our thinking, but allow His will to permeate our being, following the instructions of the apostle Paul:

> Do not conform any longer to the pattern of this world, but be transformed by the renewing of your mind. Then you will be able to test and approve what God's will is— his good, pleasing and perfect will.
>
> —ROMANS 12:2

Christ can renew our minds. His transforming power helps us replace negative, worldly thoughts and imaginations with His eternal wisdom. We are able to look to Jesus and focus on His love, His peace, His thanksgiving, and His forgiveness. Again, the word for this renewal is *metanoia*—a changed mind, a transformed mind.

When we give up the mind of the world to have the mind of

Christ, we are at peace because we are satisfied with Jesus. We no longer need the world because we walk in the power of the Holy Spirit, rather than trying to live directing our own way. Yet selfishness remains the root of so many of our struggles and problems. Consider God's lament through His prophet, Jeremiah, over the people of Israel caused by selfishness:

> My people have committed two sins: They have forsaken me, the spring of living water, and have dug their own cisterns, broken cisterns that cannot hold water.
> —JEREMIAH 2:13

God reproaches the people of Israel through His prophet, Jeremiah, for turning away from Him. They turned from worshiping the living God, the "fountain of life" (Psalm 36:9) to worshiping idols, which was like trying to create their own water. Symbolically, they were seeking a source of life that excluded God. In a practical sense, they built their own cisterns for water. But those cisterns didn't work. When the people went to them for water, all they found was mud and muck. When they went to the idols for spiritual water, they came away empty because the idols were false gods.

The people's selfishness ended up hurting them. The cisterns raised false hopes about drinkable water. The idols offered empty promises. Their selfishness was the opposite of faith. They no longer trusted God to provide and thought they needed to take care of themselves. As a result, they found themselves isolated from God.

At what times are we selfish? We may not need cisterns to provide drinking water, but do we envision ourselves relying on our own "spring of living water" to sustain us? How often do we turn from a mind-set of trusting in God to imaginations of selfishness?

One of Frank Sinatra's most famous songs is entitled "My Way." The song's lyrics talk about a person making his own choices, not following someone else's rules. One of Sinatra's nicknames was the "Chairman of the Board." In his life he certainly made up his own rules as he went along, for better or worse. And he developed quite a reputation for being in charge.

Now think about this philosophy in relationship to God. God needs to be the "Chairman of the Board" in our life. And we have to desire to live His way, not our way. When we fall away from following God's directions and from godly ideas, we are arrogant. Then we follow our own desires and engage in ungodly actions. Our arrogance can lead to self-destruction. According to the Scriptures, arrogance is one of the most ungodly characteristics, and we must overcome it:

> There are six things the LORD hates, seven that are detestable to him: haughty eyes, a lying tongue, hands that shed innocent blood, a heart that devises wicked schemes, feet that are quick to rush into evil, a false witness who pours out lies and a man who stirs up dissension among brothers.
>
> —PROVERBS 6:16–19

This is a very vivid description of what God hates. If we are motivated by our desire for control, our arrogance that we can live "our way" without the Word of God, this wrong motivation leads our hearts and our imaginations away from Him. We have lost our firm footing of faith in God's promises. In our arrogance, we rebel against the Word of God. We cannot find genuine satisfaction until we reject the desire to control our own lives and remember His promises to provide for us. We need to remember His eternal promises:

> "For I know the plans I have for you," declares the LORD, "plans to prosper you and not to harm you, plans to give you hope and a future."
>
> —JEREMIAH 29:11

There is an Old Testament story about an arrogant king who wanted to be in control. King Nebuchadnezzar was a brilliant military tactician, skilled in international diplomacy. During his reign, the Chaldean empire flourished. He even rebuilt the city of Babylon. With its paved roads, canals, and temples, the city was magnificent.

Nebuchadnezzar occupied Judah, including Jerusalem, deporting King Jehoiakim to Babylon. He also took hostages, including Daniel, back to Babylon. Then one day, as King Nebuchadnezzar was walking on the roof of his palace, his pride got the better of him, and he said:

> "Is not this the great Babylon I have built as the royal residence, by my mighty power and for the glory of my majesty?" The words were still on his lips when a voice came from heaven, "This is what is decreed for you, King Nebuchadnezzar: Your royal authority has been taken from you. You will be driven away from people and will live with the wild animals; you will eat grass like cattle. Seven times will pass by for you until you acknowledge that the Most High is sovereign over the kingdoms of men and gives them to anyone he wishes."
>
> —DANIEL 4:30–32

The king wanted to take credit for all the good things of his kingdom. God's punishment of the earthly king's imaginations of pride and control was swift. Nebuchadnezzar lost his honor as a king and as a man. He lost his kingdom, his subjects, and his reason. He became like an animal, running wild on all fours in the fields and woods. The one who thought he was greater than the average person was made to be less, eating grass like animals.

Nebuchadnezzar was insecure and selfish. We lose, too, because of our pride when we have imaginations of being in control.

It is easy for us to start taking the credit for all the blessings we have and all our accomplishments and activities and awards. As a doctor, it is easy for me to say, "Oh, look what I've accomplished! Look how many people I've helped. Look at this great medical practice I have built."

It is easy for people in any profession, and it is human nature, to want to take pride in our accomplishments. But to do so makes us lose sight of God's sovereignty and His power in helping us achieve success in our life. We may think we have done great things by our own power and think of ourselves as powerful. Our pride and arrogance bring us down.

That is what happened to this arrogant king. But there is good news in the story of Nebuchadnezzar. God didn't leave the king running wild in the fields. Nebuchadnezzar recovered his senses; his sanity was restored. No longer did he look down to the earth to provide for him, as an animal does. No longer did pride and arrogance motivate him. He lifted his eyes up as a man to heaven, as a humble petitioner for God's mercy, and saw the glory and majesty of the eternal God who rules over us all. He praised God, saying:

> [God's] dominion is an eternal dominion; His kingdom endures from generation to generation. All the peoples of the earth are regarded as nothing. He does as he pleases with the powers of heaven and the peoples of the earth. No one can hold back his hand or say to him: "What have you done?"
>
> —Daniel 4:34–35

Nebuchadnezzar humbled himself and glorified God. Then he was restored as king, with added wisdom. He more fully understood that only God is in control, and Nebuchadnezzar praised and honored the King of heaven.

We need to do the same. We can find our complete satisfaction in God's promises. He has all the power. We can do all things through Him when we find ourselves in Him. However, we will not be perfect as we struggle to surrender ourselves every day to His control. We will sometimes be tempted by vain imaginations.

As with Nebuchadnezzar, it is important that we are able to admit when we have done wrong. I once broke a leg skiing. I just had to admit I was going too fast and had my binding too tight.

I paid dearly for wanting the thrill of going fast and catching up with my buddies.

We have to admit our wrong motivation and sinful desires. We must say, "Lord, I'm way off track in the way my mind is aligned to earthly things. Align me to Jesus." And we also need to let go of the past—our successes as well as our shortcomings, our fears about failure, the consequences of sin in our life, our unmet needs, our unresolved feelings and memories, our rejections. Dwelling on past history distorts our patterns of thinking and doesn't allow His perfect vision complete access to our thoughts.

As we fix our imaginations on an attitude of surrender, we need to dedicate our mind to surrendering to God. In King David's last recorded words, he said:

> Is not my house right with God? Has he not made with me an everlasting covenant, arranged and secured in every part? Will he not bring to fruition my salvation and grant me my every desire? But evil men are all to be cast aside like thorns, which are not gathered with the hand.
>
> —2 SAMUEL 23:5–6

In these verses, King David was expressing his disappointment that his family did not love and serve God as much as they should have. David anticipated there would be trouble in his family after his death. But God's love had changed David. David knew that love could change others, if they surrendered to God. How much more difficult it would be for his family if they continued to rebel against the one and only God.

It is true for us today. We can never realize God's transforming love if we are motivated by our own rebellion. Yet David also knew that he had a covenant with God. And like King David, those of us who receive God's forgiveness and pass it on, who receive God's *agape* love and pass it on, and who receive Jesus and pass Him on—have a covenant.

Now, there are people who go to church, who love the church, who do all kinds of good deeds for the church and in the name of the church. They go to the Lord and say they are sorry for their sin. But they continue to commit the same sin without a changed mind. And again, they have to go back to the Lord and say they are sorry.

Saying we are sorry is not enough. We have to live out our repentance in a visibly changed heart and a changed life to truly feel the power of God in us. It is OK to feel remorse when we have sinned, when we have made a mistake. But remorse is not enough. We need to truly repent of our sin, which involves turning from it. Then we need to return our mind to Him and let Christlike thoughts direct our actions. We are what we think. We have not fully repented unless our actions reflect a God-centered mind.

Paul understood this reality when he declared to King Agrippa:

> So then, King Agrippa, I was not disobedient to the vision from heaven. First to those in Damascus, then to those in Jerusalem and in all Judea, and to the Gentiles also, I preached that they should repent and turn to God and prove their repentance by their deeds.
>
> —ACTS 26:19–20

Remember. Repent. Return. This process is the essence of Christianity. When we stray from our sense of satisfaction in Him and try to create our own satisfaction in worldly terms, we must choose this process. When we try to do it our own way, we need to remember, then repent and return to God. In that way we acknowledge that our true satisfaction is found only in an eternal relationship with the person of Jesus Christ.

> Remember the height from which you have fallen! Repent and do the things you did at first.
>
> —REVELATION 2:5

When we fail, we must first remember our true foundation: the power of transforming faith in the promises of God. Then, in faith, we repent of our sins. And then we return to living a life that glorifies God, in our thoughts as well as in our actions.

Repentance is turning toward Christ, not just turning away from the world. We have no eternal life until we meet God and trust Him and submit ourselves to the Lordship of Christ. Eternal life springs from repentance to God and learning to live in His presence.

What a dynamic imagination! Turning ourselves, focusing ourselves fully on the redeeming power of Christ's blood and His ultimate sacrifice for each of us. Hear His promise:

> The Lord is not slow in keeping his promise, as some understand slowness. He is patient with you, not wanting anyone to perish, but everyone to come to repentance.
>
> —2 PETER 3:9

God wants each of us to repent and turn to Him! He offers salvation to all. He knows we will perish without Him. Life truly begins when we surrender to Christ at Calvary, when we marvel at God's matchless grace. Only then do we find true satisfaction. Only then do we realize that the power of the resurrection is ours for eternity!

The good news is that we can pursue the mind of God every day! We can claim our eternal life in Him every day! We can live before the Lord Jesus, our King, and let Him be our joy and portion, our King and Master.

May each of us let go of our selfishness and cling to Christ, surrendering our lives to Him with abandon. As we remember, repent, and return, our new, surrendered selves live with Him. And we learn to live in the power of the resurrection, the love of the Trinity, and His presence for eternity!

CHAPTER 10

Resting in God

THE KEY PRINCIPLE TO STAYING focused on God is to be faithful to keep His eternal perspective before us every day. This is impossible to do if we think we must rely solely on our own self-discipline. So imagine maintaining this attitude another way, by receiving the mind of Christ. Then we can see how He works to transform us. We can see how the Holy Spirit infuses us and engulfs our hearts and minds with His eternal perspective.

When we take on the mind of Christ, much of life's struggle is resolved and we are able to truly rest in Him. We still face difficulties, trials, and temptations. But we can trust in Him, lean on Him, rely on Him, depend on Him, and rest in Him at all times. In receiving the mind of Christ, we have the true images of Him as Jehovah-Jireh, as our Father, as our Shepherd, as the one who provides.

One of the most important attitudes of the mind is to be totally surrendered to God, and yet totally concentrated on Him. It sounds like a paradox. Let me give you some examples. In golf, a player must fully concentrate on the game, yet be totally relaxed so the body performs well. If your wrist is too tight when you swing the club, your wrist will not move correctly. When you hit the ball it doesn't go very far; sometimes it does not even go in the right direction.

In the operating room, a doctor must concentrate on the procedure. But if he or she is worried and nervous and uptight, the operation will seem more difficult to perform. In skiing, the term for this concentrated mind-set is anticipation. You have to concentrate to go safely down the hill, but you also have to trust your skills and gravity to bring you through the turns safely to the bottom. You anticipate the turn, plant your pole, pull your body, and surrender to the forces of gravity and your own reflexes, which bring you through the turn. When I am skiing, I go down the slopes with my wife, praying, "Lord, let us surrender, surrender, surrender." We surrender as we go down the hill.

The only way to truly relax through life's turns is to be surrendered to God. It is His will that guides our lives. We live through Him and for Him. We align ourselves with Him. Consider how Paul's attitude exemplifies this:

> I have been crucified with Christ and I no longer live, but Christ lives in me. The life I live in the body, I live by faith in the Son of God, who loved me and gave himself for me.
>
> —GALATIANS 2:20

No longer do we act solely through our own efforts. We let the Lord's strength and vision guide us. We keep our eyes on the goal: getting down the slope or living the life of Christ. Living in anticipation in Christ, we have to look into His eyes, drop our bodies down, and let God-given strength empower us. We need to let the power of God's gravity pull us through as we plant our poles. Then we get the automatic spring as we come through and turn into the fall line. The next turn spontaneously takes place, with no effort.

In skiing, there is no effort at all when the proper technique is used: anticipating, planting the pole, letting gravity pull you into the hill around the turn—and relaxing through all the motion. If you don't relax, your muscles get tense and don't stay flexible. That is when you fall. As Christians, we must not allow ourselves to be tense in life. We must stay relaxed. Our satisfaction in God's promise to provide gives us this attitude, imagination, and mind-set.

When we have surrendered completely to our "pole plant,"

we rise up with total faith that He will continually provide for us. When we rest in the Lord and totally relinquish ourselves, we are at peace with our God, ourselves, our work, and others. It requires being able to trust, being thankful, and believing. We then are amazed at the strength God gives us. We are truly enabled to live by faith and die to self. Look again at the apostle Paul's "anticipation" of life:

> I have been crucified with Christ and I no longer live, but Christ lives in me. The life I live in the body, I live by faith in the Son of God, who loved me and gave himself for me.
>
> —GALATIANS 2:20

We plant the pole: "I have been crucified with Christ." We give in to His gravity, His power, His pressure: "Christ lives in me." He is the point of reference for our bodies, our minds, our muscles, our decisions. Our thoughts are His thoughts. His will is our will. As we plant the pole, we rise up and live in this flesh by faith. We make the turn, fulfilling Galatians 2:20: "I live by faith in the Son of God, who loved me and gave himself for me."

When we work together in a joyous rhythm of enjoyment in life in Christ, even our bodies can be at peace, totally relaxed in doing everything through God's power. Unfortunately we don't always live according to Galatians 2:20. I know a man whose life was the opposite of this rest in Christ. He was the manager of a very important corporation. He believed and practiced Christian ethics in business and was completely trustworthy. Yet he didn't know how to relax. He wasn't able to enjoy life. He was the perfect example of a good body being destroyed by a brain that wasn't allowing the body to function as it should.

In life we need to simply rise up with God's strength, knowing and believing the Lord will complete everything He has started, including the unexpected "turns" in our lives. Our Lord gives us a beautiful image that illustrates how we should rest in Him:

I am the true vine, and my Father is the gardener. He
cuts off every branch in me that bears no fruit, while
every branch that does bear fruit he prunes so that it
will be even more fruitful. You are already clean because
of the word I have spoken to you. Remain in me, and I
will remain in you. No branch can bear fruit by itself;
it must remain in the vine. Neither can you bear fruit
unless you remain in me.

—JOHN 15:1–4

In our minds, we need the imagination of Jesus as the vine,
nourishing us, feeding us, directing our growth. Life as a branch
is one of implicit rest. We can't push the vine, telling it where
we want to go or what we want to do. We cannot provide for
ourselves. If we are cut off from the vine, we will perish. When
we don't abide in Him, we become very barren and experiencing
"burn out" is likely. All we can do is joyfully rest in union with the
vine of life, as the Scriptures teach us to do:

Trust in the LORD with all your heart and lean not on
your own understanding; in all your ways acknowledge
him, and he will make your paths straight.

—PROVERBS 3:5

Every day, all we can do is say, "Lord, I want to depend on you
in everything I do." We need to think of ourselves as lambs, dependent for our lives on our great Shepherd, the living God. When we
rest in our relationship with the living, transforming Lord, it does
not make us slothful and lazy. To the contrary, resting in Him pro-
duces real fruit: true peace and His spirit of love and service. We
desire to be closer to Him, and we are resting in the Spirit.

We will face periods of pruning experienced as times of trouble and hardship. But our attachment to the vine, our relationship with Jesus Christ, will continue to nourish and sustain us
during those painful seasons. When we trust in the Lord and rest
in Him, we glorify Him. He gets glory and we get joy!

CHAPTER II

Communion With Christ

Is it enough to simply say that we are surrendering our wills to God? How do we know whether or not we are resting in Him? Does having an eternal view of our lives free us from daily responsibility? These questions serve to address a more basic issue: Do we think of God as a remote, distant being or is He our partner with whom we commune in daily living?

None of these other issues are meaningful unless Jesus is vibrantly in our lives every day. Surrendering our wills, learning to rest, and living with an eternal view of life as we accept daily responsibilities can have no meaning without a life of communion with Christ. Our responsibility is to continue daily in faith, for without faith there is no relationship with the living God.

> Blessed are those who have learned to acclaim you, who walk in the light of your presence, O LORD.
> —PSALM 89:15

This verse speaks of a habitual spiritual walk with God. It tells us we are blessed when we learn to have that daily relationship. In fact, there are many verses in the Bible that talk about walking with God, about believing in Jesus' presence in our lives every day. We find our full measure of satisfaction when we walk daily in that divine communion.

Several authors have described this walk with God using different images. C.S. Lewis would say we are in meaningful acceleration when we are in harmony with the character of God. John Piper would say we are glorifying God by enjoying Him forever.

Hudson Taylor would say we have a balance between being totally at peace with God and desiring to be closer to Him. Jonathan Edwards would say our minds are aligned with God.

All those definitions describe a eucharistic lifestyle. Some churches celebrate the Eucharist as the Lord's Supper, or Communion. The eucharistic lifestyle is an imagination of the mind in which we are in continual communion with the Lord, continually in prayer with the Lord, continually worshiping and praising the Lord.

The Old Testament tells us about a man named Enoch who "walked with God; then he was no more, because God took him away" (Genesis 5:24). When Enoch was sixty-five-years-old, he became the father of Methuselah. He lived another three hundred years and had other children as well. The biblical testimony of his life is that day in and day out, year in and year out, for more than three hundred years he walked with God.

We can only conclude that on his down days, Enoch sought God's help for encouragement in his disappointments with life. On his up days, he praised God for His great goodness. God was the essence of his life. Enoch had a personal relationship with God. They were in constant fellowship. Then Enoch was translated into the presence of God because he walked in His steps and grew intimate with Him.

> By faith Enoch was taken away so that he did not see death; "and was not found because God had taken him"; for before he was taken he had this testimony, that he pleased God.
>
> —HEBREWS 11:5, NKJV

Do we have a habit of walking with God? Or just talking at Him? When we are intimate with the Lord Jesus, we fellowship with Him. We renew our minds, especially through daily prayer and the study of His Word, which transforms us into His image in all areas of our lives.

Bible knowledge is important, but more important is satisfaction with the person of Jesus Christ in our lives. Praise is important, but more important is satisfaction with the person of Jesus Christ in our life. Prayer is important, but more important is satisfaction with the person of Jesus Christ in our lives.

Satisfaction comes through a relationship, through daily communion with God. He wants an intimate relationship of love with us. And Christ is the key to that intimacy. Through Christ we have a relationship with our Creator. We know God through Christ, and through Christ we are known to God. We must become as a child seeking His heart. Our relationship with God is one of surrender and a desire to have intimate fellowship with Him until we are engulfed in, and intertwined with, His presence. Then we enter into the fullness of God!

I know God as the one who saves the worst of sinners. Every day I strive to keep Him intimately involved in every aspect of my life. He totally intertwines the past, the present, and the future. He holds all the forces of the universe in the palm of His hand. Christ demonstrated that power by being nailed on the cross, carrying all the sins of the world. Jesus Christ, the only sinless soul, died for all my sins and all of your sins.

It is important that we do not think of God according to some small, remote concept of one who created the world, sent Jesus to save it, and now observes us from a distance. God is within us and around us. He gives us a future to believe in. He allows us to do all things through that same Christ who suffered and died on the cross and now lives to redeem and strengthen us.

Think about the first time you fell in love. Remember that initial glow, that feeling of walking on air because you loved someone? Maybe that person loved you in return, maybe not. But your life was changed because you were in love. The air you breathed was different, food tasted different, your sleep patterns changed, everything about you and around you seemed different because you were in love.

Now, think about how those feelings changed as the two of

you developed a relationship. What happened? Did the love grow stronger? Did the passion burn brighter? Did you grow more committed to that person? Or, as you grew to know him or her better, did you become less interested, until the relationship withered away?

Let's apply this to our relationship with God. I have seen many people who fall head over heels in love with God when He first touches their hearts. Their faces shine; they have a different kind of glow. Others are transformed quietly, subtly, but they love Him deeply. The psalmist described this phenomenon:

> Those who look to him are radiant; their faces are never covered with shame.
>
> —PSALM 34:5

When God first touches us and we surrender to Him, we take the first step on the path to an eternal relationship of love. Christ saves us, making us new creatures. However, it is our mind-set from that point that determines our relationship with Him.

I once heard the Reverend Larry Jackson of Clinton, North Carolina, preach about our relationship with Christ. He asked the question, "Are we married to Jesus or are we just trying to 'shack up' with Him?" Think about the implications. Are we passionate about Christ or are we halfhearted about our love for Him? Are we committed to Christ or do we just enjoy the relationship until we find some other interest? Are we trying to get something for nothing out of this relationship or are we interested in surrendering ourselves to it? Have we changed where we live? Have we changed our name? Do we want to know more about Christ or are we reluctant to devote time to build the relationship?

Godly imaginations of the mind can only be developed in a deeply personal relationship with God. It is almost like getting married and then learning what married life is all about. Our satisfaction in Christ and our imaginations of Him are developing daily. But underneath is the desire for a relationship with Him more than anything else. The daily development may be fast or slow, but it becomes a reality because we are faithfully and fervently focused on Him. Isaiah declared:

> You will keep in perfect peace him whose mind is steadfast, because he trusts in you.
>
> —ISAIAH 26:3

A *steadfast* mind is another way of describing imaginations that are focused on God. It is a mind that is intertwined with the mind of Christ. We meditate on God's presence and praise Him, talk with Him, and listen to Him. It is another way of saying that we worship Him. Worship is the greatest expression of intimacy with God, who lives in our hearts. And as we live in communion with Him every day, the result of that intimacy is perfect peace.

We need to be in constant worship of God—worshiping Him for who He is and for what He has done and will do for us. Worship needs to be integrated into our normal behavior, our family, our work—into all of life. The essence of worship is not an external action, going to a church service once a week to sing some songs and listen to a religious message. Rather, it is an internal, intense imagination of constant love, praise, and thanksgiving. It is daily communion with our Creator, Redeemer, and Sustainer! This kind of relationship builds trust in a faithful God:

> Those who know your name will trust in you, for you, LORD, have never forsaken those who seek you.
>
> —PSALM 9:10

In the Bible, many words are used to identify God and to name Him. Each of these names reveals a different aspect of the God with whom we walk every day. They help us gain a greater understanding of the eternal God with whom we have an intimate relationship. Here we find images of God that can guide our thoughts and help us worship Him. Here we see His promises unfold. Let's examine a few of these names of God to see what they reveal about His nature. He is first revealed to us in creation:

> In the beginning God created the heavens and the earth.
> —GENESIS 1:1

The Hebrew word for God here is *Elohim*, the Eternal Creator who always was and always will be. Elohim is the God of power who created all and controls all, yet remains separate from His creation, as an artist from a painting. Elohim is a plural noun in form but has a singular meaning. It speaks of His nature. Our imagination of Elohim is the one who exists beyond the boundaries of time, who with His almighty power created everything.

> …the LORD God made the earth and the heavens.
> —GENESIS 2:4

Here the word *Lord* is used with God, which, in the Hebrew is *Jehovah-Elohim*. Jehovah is the great and incommunicable Name of God. When it is combined with Elohim, the name means a God, not just of power, but of perfection—a finishing God. We imagine Jehovah-Elohim as the Self-Existent one who gives life to all beings.

> I am God Almighty; walk before me and be blameless. I will confirm my covenant between me and you and will greatly increase your numbers."
> —GENESIS 17:1–2

The term *El Shaddai*—God Almighty or All-Sufficient—was used when God established His covenant with Abraham. By using this name, God pledges that He will strengthen and satisfy His people. Abraham will be fruitful, but it will be fruit carefully tended and purified. God will strengthen His people as a father strengthens a child—by meeting their needs and chastening them for their own good. Then they will flourish. Through Him they will be strong. Imagine El Shaddai as our strength, our source of comfort, our nourishment, our confidence, and our satisfaction. He is All-Sufficient. We need nothing more.

> So Abraham called that place The LORD Will Provide. And to this day it is said, "On the mountain of the LORD it will be provided."
>
> —GENESIS 22:14

The Lord who will provide is *Jehovah-Jireh.* Following God's command, Abraham had taken Isaac into the mountains to kill him as a sacrifice to God. Abraham had been faithful to God. He had given up all that God had asked—his country and kindred, his nephew, Lot, his plans for his son, Ishmael, and now his son, Isaac. He built the altar, tied up Isaac, and placed him on the wood. As he pulled out his knife to kill his son, an angel intervened and saved Isaac. God provided another sacrifice that day, a ram that had been caught in some bushes. And hundreds of years later He provided another sacrifice for the whole world, His only Son, who died for all our sins. Imagine God as a loving Father, providing His Son as a sacrifice for each of us.

> …I am the LORD, who heals you.
>
> —EXODUS 15:26

Jehovah-Rapha, the Lord our Healer, not only offers physical healing, but the healing of our souls as well. Jesus explains salvation in simple terms in Matthew 9:12, when He says, "It is not the healthy who need a doctor, but the sick." Our souls are sick until we find satisfaction in Him. For believers who put their trust in Him, Christ continues to be the Great Physician. When we stray from a perfect vision of Him and our thoughts no longer reflect Him, we must come to Him for renewed healing. If we do not, the sickness in our souls will first weaken, then deform and destroy us. But God is faithful, and He promises to heal us. He brings us back to Himself, heals our souls, and fills us with His satisfaction. Let this wonderful reality fill our imaginations.

> Moses built an altar and called it The LORD is my Banner.
> —EXODUS 17:15

Soldiers on the battlefield used to fly a flag or banner. The banner showed them which way to go in the heat of battle, and it gave them a symbol around which they could rally. It became a source of pride, identity, and inspiration. *Jehovah-Nissi* was the banner for the Israelites. And Isaiah describes the coming Messiah as, "a banner for the peoples; the nations will rally to him, and his place of rest will be glorious" (Isaiah 11:10). The Lord is our Banner, our inspiration, our encouragement, our symbol, and our guide.

> So Gideon built an altar to the LORD there and called it The LORD is Peace.
> —JUDGES 6:24

Gideon felt little internal peace. God had called him to deliver the Israelites from the oppressive rule of the Midianites. Gideon did not want the job because he did not think he was up to the task, and he did not have much faith that God would give him victory. Finally, he asked for a sign, preparing an offering of meat and bread. The angel of the Lord touched it and fire consumed it. Then Gideon understood that it was God calling him, and his heart was at peace.

Our hearts can find the same peace of *Jehovah-Shalom* when we remember He is calling us. He will give us the tools we need to fulfill His calling. He is our peace in all circumstances. He is the ultimate image of peace.

> This is the name by which he will be called: The LORD Our Righteousness.
> —JEREMIAH 23:6

In this prophecy, Jeremiah explains that the Messiah will be *Jehovah-Tsidkenu*, the Lord Our Righteousness. Through His death on the cross, He is the one through whom we obtain righteousness. He is the Lord, who makes us right with God. He is our Savior, because His death on the cross gives us His righteousness in exchange for our sins.

> And the name of the city from that time on will be: The LORD is There.
>
> —EZEKIEL 48:35

Jehovah-Shammah, The Lord is There, reveals His abiding presence with His people. God told Moses, "My Presence will go with you" (Exodus 33:14). David wrote, "You will fill me with joy in your presence" (Psalm 16:11). Jesus promised, "And surely I am with you always, to the very end of the age" (Matthew 28:20). There is no greater comfort and satisfaction than to know that He is always with us.

> The LORD Almighty—he is the King of glory.
>
> —PSALM 24:10

Jehovah-Sabaoth, the Lord Almighty, can also be translated as the Lord of Hosts. The Hebrew word for *hosts* is *tsaba*[1] and is used in this verse as a special reference to an assembled army for warfare. The same word is used to refer to heavenly bodies (Genesis 2:1; Nehemiah 9:6; Isaiah 40:26) and angels (Luke 2:13). As Jehovah-Sabaoth, God is able to make His omnipotent power known. He can marshal all the hosts of heaven to fulfill His purposes and to help His people. We find confidence in this name, knowing that He is our help and our strength.

> Say to the Israelites, 'You must observe my Sabbaths. This will be a sign between me and you for the genera-

tions to come, so you may know that I am the LORD, who makes you holy.'

—EXODUS 31:13

Jehovah-M'kaddesh, the Lord who makes us holy, sets us apart as a holy people of His own for His service. It is the Lord who sanctifies us and makes us holy. We cannot achieve such a standard on our own. "But you were washed, you were sanctified, you were justified in the name of the Lord Jesus Christ and by the Spirit of our God" (1 Corinthians 6:11). His blood sets us apart; His blood makes us holy; His blood distinguishes us.

> Come, let us bow down in worship, let us kneel before the LORD our Maker; for he is our God and we are the people of his pasture, the flock under his care.
>
> —PSALM 95:6–7

We have a personal relationship with *Jehovah-Oseenu*, the Lord our Maker. He made each of us, and as our personal Creator, He has a right to our lives. Others may kneel down and worship gods and idols of their own making, but our God made us. We worship Him because He gives us life, and He preserves and protects us every day.

> How awesome is the LORD Most High, the great King over all the earth!
>
> —PSALM 47:2

The Lord Most High, *El Elyon*, is the Creator and Ruler of earth. He is the rightful owner and Lord over all the creatures because He made them. What a wonderful image of God as the highest ruling authority. When we belong to Him, He will protect us. He is the greatest King and Highest Lord.

In these verses, we have seen God as our eternal and personal Creator, the one who gives us life, who heals us, meets all our needs, and gives us peace. He is always with us. He is our righteousness;

73

He sanctifies us and makes us holy. Each of us can focus our thoughts and imaginations on these promises of God. We can know, in our heads and in our hearts, that He is deeply committed and involved with each of us. He has promised that eternal commitment to us through the names he uses to reveal Himself to us.

In the Old Testament, as we have seen, God is our Creator who made us. We bow before Him and revere Him as our Maker. He saves us and protects us. He is transcendent, above us. He is eternal, unchangeable, and without limits. He is independent and self-existent. God is infinitely greater than all His creatures and infinite in holiness. God's transcendence is His greatness. These images reveal God's ability to create and sustain all the intricacies of the universe. They also reveal God as deeply and intimately concerned about each of us.

In the New Testament, God reveals Himself in a new way—He comes to mankind as the person of Jesus Christ. Christ is the path to the Father, our Creator, our Almighty, our Healer, our Banner, our constant Provider. He is immanent—near to us as our help and comfort. God becomes man to be our Redeemer. He is with us and we are in union with Him.

> So it is written: "The first man Adam became a living being;" the last Adam, a life-giving spirit.
> —1 CORINTHIANS 15:45

Jesus is the second Adam, who came to earth to redeem mankind from sin. In many myths of the ancient world, gods came down and dwelt among men. For example, the Greeks believed that their gods lived with men and when men did foolish things, the gods began to despise them. However, Christianity differs from these myths in that the Lord Jesus is the great transcendent God who came down and lived among men and loved them to the degree of giving His life for their sins.

God exalted him to his own right hand as Prince and
Savior that he might give repentance and forgiveness of
sins to Israel.

—ACTS 5:31

Jesus gives forgiveness to all who seek it in faith and repentance. That should be our overriding image of Him. Jesus' purpose is to bring us to Himself and then to the Father. In our
normal human state, we turn to the world's values and perspective of life. But Jesus provides our way for turning away from
the world and turning to God. When we accept Jesus as our
Savior, we find our place with Him, the one who is at the right
hand of God.

Imagine the privilege and power in simply calling on His
name. Peter and Paul were able to accomplish amazing miracles
in the name of Jesus. We can do the same. We can call on His
name to cast out false imaginations. We can use His name to help
us focus our thoughts, to bring the proper balance in our life. As
Jesus brought everything under total submission to His Father, so
we must bring everything under total submission to God—in the
name of Jesus Christ.

Jesus has the power to change our lives at this very moment—
He is the power of peace, and the power of wisdom, knowledge,
and discernment. Jesus is the key to our eternal relationship
with God.

Remember, our imaginations today shape our eternity. Every
day we need to begin with a fresh commitment to our relationship with Christ. Every day we need to focus our imaginations
on finding satisfaction in Christ. Every day we need to renew our
communion with the Lord. Every day we need to worship Him.

I delight greatly in the LORD; my soul rejoices in my
God. For he has clothed me with garments of salvation
and arrayed me in a robe of righteousness.

—ISAIAH 61:10

This is the God with whom Enoch walked. This is the God in whom Paul rested and found contentment. This is the God who can clothe us in salvation and righteousness! In our imaginations, we need to see ourselves in union with Him, knowing Him as we are known (1 Corinthians 13:12). Worshiping and walking with the Lord every day will transform our lives because it places Him at the center of our hearts. Then we find true satisfaction.

Hope, faith, peace, and love are united in our souls as we become one with Christ and He becomes one with us. Our actions are guided by our love for Him and faith in His promises. True love, joy, and peace are ours—now and for eternity!

CHAPTER 12

Filled With Thanksgiving

Two men were sitting in a cafeteria eating lunch. As they began to eat, the first said to the second, "Is something wrong? Do you feel sick?" The second said, "No. What do you mean?" The first replied, "Oh, your head was down." "I was just giving thanks to the Lord," the second man responded. The first man asked, "You believe in all that stuff? I just start right in when I eat." The second answered, "I understand. My dog does the same thing."

So often we can act just like dogs—jumping in without thanking God for all His blessing in our life. At times we begin to think that we can take the credit for our house, our car, our family. But God has provided it all. We need to be thankful for our daily strength and activities and health, our relationships, our work, even our ability to laugh. That imagination of thanksgiving is essential to a life of genuine worship.

Communion with God is real and meaningful when we are thankful to God. We walk with God genuinely when we appreciate His majesty, His person in Christ, the joy of His living in our hearts, and the promise of being engulfed with Him forever.

A basic element of our relationship with God is a state of thanksgiving. We could call it a "thanksgiving frenzy", which exudes from every inch of our body as we go to work, perform household chores, get up in the morning, and go to bed at night. We need to live in a state of constant thanksgiving.

> Give thanks in all circumstances, for this is God's will for you in Christ Jesus.
>
> —1 THESSALONIANS 5:18

> Always giving thanks to God the Father for everything,
> in the name of our Lord Jesus Christ.
> —EPHESIANS 5:20

A thankful spirit is the basic motivation for our faith, our love, and our surrender to God. When we are truly thankful, it is because we realize who God is and how sinful we are.

Joel Fish, a sports psychologist, says we must develop a friendly, thankful mind when we participate in sports activities. Many golfers crack their clubs, slam clubs into the ground, and even throw clubs when they're frustrated about their game. Those golfers have not developed a thankful attitude about the game. When golf is played with thanksgiving, joy, and exuberance, performance excels.

During long races in which I would run twenty-four to thirty hours, I did not think about myself. I did not concentrate on the aches and pains, the course ahead, or how I had performed to that point. I did not look down, I did not look back, I did not even look ahead. I looked up. I quoted Scriptures, I sang songs praising God, and I was thankful for the opportunity to be in the race and for the ability He had given me to participate.

When I concentrated on being thankful, I did not have time and energy to notice the aches and pains that cropped up during a race. When we turn our imaginations to thanking God in all the areas of our lives, our minds are focused on Him. It is more difficult for worldly imaginations and negative attitudes to gain a foothold in our minds. A thankful spirit helps us control all our imaginations.

> Through Jesus, therefore, let us continually offer to God a
> sacrifice of praise—the fruit of lips that confess his name.
> —HEBREWS 13:15

But we must guard against thanking God only for our possessions and ourselves. If we are thankful merely for the possessions we have, we may be violating the pure beauty of the worship of thanksgiving. When we are expressing gratitude as a mere formality, or to make us feel good, or to take us away from our worries, we really are not worshiping God.

Our hearts should overflow with thanksgiving for the person of Jesus Christ living in us. We should be filled with thanksgiving for knowing that we have a Savior who has saved us from our sins and should rejoice continually that the Lord has taken our confessed sin and accepted our repentance. We need to live in a state of thanksgiving to God, seeing His work in our lives every minute, every day, giving thanks for His sovereignty, His love, His grace.

This ecstasy of thanksgiving comes when we realize that He is within us and will be with us forever. The greatest joy comes from being intertwined with the presence of God now and knowing that it will extend throughout eternity!

Chapter 13

An Eternal Relationship

Think back to some relationships you have had with parents, friends, spouses, and children. What makes some relationships successful? Why do some struggle?

Robert J. Sternberg, a professor of psychology and education at Yale University, says a love relationship is built on passion, intimacy, and commitment. These elements form a "love triangle" between two people. These same elements apply to our relationship with God.

Passion

Do we seek God out of a sense of obligation? Or do we search after Him with real desire as a deer pants for the brook? That is the way the psalmist describes longing for God:

> As the deer pants for streams of water, so my soul pants for you, O God. My soul thirsts for God, for the living God.
> —Psalm 42:1–2

In Jesus' day there was a pool of water in Bethesda believed to have healing powers. Jesus appeared to one man at the pool and asked, "Do you want to get well?" (John 5:6). He wanted to know that man's desire. Did he truly desire to be healed? Or was he there because others had told him to go there? What was his inner desire?

Christ wants to know the truth in each of us. Do we have a passion, a drive, a hope, a longing, a desire for intimacy with Christ?

Even Paul, who wrote so eloquently about being content, said he wanted to know the Lord better and better (Philippians 3:10).

Being married to Christ gives us a new focus, a new orientation, a new desire. In our new imaginations we passionately seek Christ. Now and for eternity. We are energized just thinking about the name of Jesus.

It is easy for us to become complacent. It is easy for us to become indifferent to God, imagining nothing rather than focusing on Him. It is easy to lose our intense passion for Christ. To avoid that difficulty, let us praise the Lord with our whole being. Let us hold on firmly to Him. Let us love Him, passionately and deeply, every day, with every thought and with every action. Imagine your life when God permeates every feeling, every thought, every action, and your zeal for His presence fills your heart and mind. That emotion is from the wonder and worship of Him.

A speaker at a Promise Keepers meeting asked this question: "Have you ever had a relationship outside of marriage that was exotic and fascinating?" Then he paused and amended the question, "In your mind?" Perhaps many of us would have to admit that we have been tempted in our imaginations.

Now apply that question to your relationship with God. Is your imagination filled with thoughts of God? Or have you found worldly desires and fantasies creeping into your imaginations? Have you strayed from your longing for God?

As humans, we are frail and feeble beings who struggle to keep our desire for God strong, but are often lured by the material goods and attitudes of the world. We can lose sight of God's almighty power and wisdom when we fantasize about our own importance and our own abilities.

We may think we have great knowledge. We may think we can control many elements of our life. But in truth, we know very little—and can control even less. We can never fully understand the simplest cell or the most grandiose parts of our universe. We have nothing worthwhile without our Creator, our Redeemer, our Sustainer. Listen to the psalmist express His passion for God:

> O God, you are my God, earnestly I seek you; my soul
> thirsts for you, my body longs for you, in a dry and weary
> land where there is no water. I have seen you in the sanc-
> tuary and beheld your power and your glory.
>
> —PSALM 63:1–2

The writers of the psalms knew that God set the universe in motion. And that He watches over each of us. Their response: to worship and love this Almighty God.

We can do no less. We need to deeply desire God, feeling His presence living within us and transforming our imaginations. We can be so deeply in love with Him that we don't fantasize about worldly possessions or goals. We find our perfect contentment in Him.

A word of caution—we must guard against that worship becoming a response of our own emotions. We cannot generate the Lord's presence in us by being emotional. We need to let godly emotion radiate from us. With the psalmist, let us cry:

> My soul yearns, even faints, for the courts of the LORD;
> my heart and my flesh cry out for the living God.
>
> —PSALM 84:2

May each of us be lovers of God! May the Spirit quicken us, so that we have hope and belief in all the promises of God, and may His Word become real within our lives. Let us cry out and seek an intimate relationship with Him, so that He is with us, He is in us, and He is seen through us!

INTIMACY

The second side of Sternberg's love triangle is *intimacy*, or "knowing." In both Hebrew and Greek, the word translated as "to know" implies a relationship most closely related to intimacy in the marriage relationship. We reveal our deepest thoughts, feelings, and fears. We are willing to risk rejection as we seek an intimate relationship. We also open our hearts to one another, revealing ourselves.

We have to know God—not just know about Him, but know Him personally. We can know all about basketball superstar Michael Jordan, but we do not know him personally. It is only through a personal relationship that we get to know someone. We have to know God and know Him well. The New Testament writers strongly agree:

> Grace and peace be yours in abundance through the knowledge of God and of Jesus our Lord.
>
> —2 Peter 1:2

> Grow in the grace and knowledge of our Lord and Savior Jesus Christ.
>
> —2 Peter 3:18

One of our greatest imaginations is understanding that we can have an intimate relationship with God. We can draw very close to Him on a personal basis, revealing our hearts and minds to Him. We must hold this image dearly.

God cries for our intimacy. He cries for us to know Him. He desires for us to understand Him and His inner workings, which have been and will be for eternity, and to know our place in those inner workings. At the same time, we must be willing to open ourselves to Him. We have to let Him tear down the defensive, protective walls we build to prevent intimacy. Hear the psalmist's cry for intimacy:

> Search me, O God, and know my heart; test me and know my anxious thoughts. See if there is any offensive way in me, and lead me in the way everlasting.
>
> —Psalm 139:23–24

The psalmist invites God to search his heart, to probe the very depths of his imaginations. He gives God complete access.

Are we willing to do that? Or are we afraid to let God into our heart completely?

We should be willing to share such perfect intimacy with our Creator. He already knows us completely. We are not really hiding anything from Him anyway. But when we invite Him to search our thoughts, it is an invitation to share our weaknesses with Him. It reveals our attitude of surrender to Him.

We give ourselves completely—all our doubts and fears, all our negative imaginations and thoughts, all our sin. We are asking God to examine our thoughts and lead us back to faith, to strengthen our faith.

To be led in the everlasting way of God we must unburden all our sins. We must allow ourselves to be engulfed in His eternal blessedness. This blessing of intimacy with God is what is promised in Numbers 6:22–27:

> The LORD said to Moses, "Tell Aaron and his sons, 'This is how you are to bless the Israelites. Say to them: The LORD bless you and keep you; the LORD make his face shine upon you and be gracious to you; the LORD turn his face toward you and give you peace.'" So they will put my name on the Israelites, and I will bless them.
>
> —NUMBERS 6:22–27

We seek the imaginations of God's blessings as each of us looks to Him. May we know His love. May we be intimate with Him. May His presence determine our ways and our steps. God promises He will bless His people. He gives His blessing to those who love Him.

COMMITMENT

The third side of the love triangle, according to Robert Sternberg, is *commitment*. How do you imagine yourself in your relationship with God? Do you see yourself as a person who can trust God, as a person who can have a relationship with God, as a person who is so committed to God that no sin can draw you away?

The story of Samson warns us what can happen when we are not fully committed to God. His example warns us not to seek satisfaction outside God's provision, when our hearts are inclined to the things of the world. Samson had been dedicated by his parents to be a Nazirite, one who is set aside to be faithful to God. He had a special calling from God: "... He will begin the deliverance of Israel from the hands of the Philistines" (Judges 13:5). Samson, a man of extraordinary strength, became a judge of Israel and led the nation for twenty years.

But Samson was a flawed leader. As a young man, he married a Philistine woman, setting off a chain of events that led to violence and the death of his wife. While in Gaza years later, he slept with a prostitute, giving the Philistines a chance to trap and kill him. He managed to escape in the middle of the night.

Then he met Delilah. Samson had not learned his lesson from previous encounters, and he fell into the same snare. He loved Delilah. But she betrayed him to the Philistines. She pleaded with him until he revealed the source of his great strength—his hair that had never been cut.

> "No razor has ever been used on my head," he said, "because I have been a Nazirite set apart to God since birth. If my head were shaved, my strength would leave me, and I would become as weak as any other man."
> —JUDGES 16:17

After he fell asleep, she summoned someone to cut his hair and delivered a weakened Samson to the rulers of the Philistines. He was now their prisoner. And he would die as their prisoner, but not before he could demonstrate once again the power of the Lord. While a prisoner, Samson's hair began to grow again. After a while, the Philistines summoned him to perform during a celebration at the temple of Dagon, the Philistines' false god, and Samson cried out to God once again:

> Then Samson reached toward the two central pillars on which the temple stood. Bracing himself against them, his right hand on the one and his left hand on the other, Samson said, "Let me die with the Philistines!" Then he pushed with all his might, and down came the temple on the rulers and all the people in it.
>
> —JUDGES 16:29–30

Samson's earthly appetites led to his downfall. Yet he was a man of mighty faith in God, who called upon Him in the darkest moments. He renewed his commitment to the Lord when he remembered the true source of strength and satisfaction.

What about us? We may have all the passion and knowledge, but do we have the commitment to stay in a relationship with the person of Jesus Christ? Commitment is essential in all relationships. Members in a business partnership are obliged to fulfill their obligations through a contract. Marriage partners pledge to remain committed to each other. Sometimes these commitments break down. Business people sue each other when contracts are broken. Spouses may divorce because one or the other wants to forget their commitment. Focusing our imagination on God will strengthen our personal commitments. The psalmist demonstrated this commitment:

> One thing I ask of the LORD, this is what I seek: that I may dwell in the house of the LORD all the days of my life, to gaze upon the beauty of the LORD and to seek him in his temple.
>
> —PSALM 27:4

Every day we need to dwell in the house of the Lord, embracing the Lord Jesus Christ. We must renew our commitment to think as God thinks. We need to have His eternal perspective, His holy attitude, His pure love.

Union with Christ

Our life as followers of Christ is where the glory of the Lord is revealed. Our part is to come close to Him, to walk along His path of life. Our whole purpose is to talk with Him in His language through prayer. We live in a state of eternal life as the Holy Spirit lives within us. In turn, He shows us the path of life:

> You have made known to me the path of life; you will fill me with joy in your presence, with eternal pleasures at your right hand.
>
> —Psalm 16:11

Our whole being seeks to unite with Him, becoming one with Him in our minds so we think with Him—we think as He thinks. That is what life is all about. It is to live in the aura, the glow, the excitement of being with the Lord. He will fill us with joy, and we will experience His eternal pleasures!

Where are we putting our investments? The most important investment we will ever make is determining how we think. Let us commit ourselves to uniting with the heart and mind of God. Let us invest our imaginations in our eternal relationship with Him!

CHAPTER 14

Soil Testing

I want to ask you a question. If you were to think of yourself as soil, what kind would you be? Are you well-worn, grooved, like a road? Do you avoid change, rejecting new ideas and approaches?

Maybe you would consider yourself to be tough, rocky soil. You are always looking out for "number one." Are you open to some new ideas, but they don't ever become a part of your life?

Or are you open to all kinds of ideas and changes? They seem to sprout up like weeds. And then you find yourself easily distracted, going in too many directions as once.

The kind of dirt that gardeners love is soil that is filled with nutrients, able to grow any flower or fruit. That kind of soil represents a person who can separate good ideas from bad ones and therefore become productive in his daily life.

Jesus used this analogy of good soil in a parable that relates to the attitude of our heart:

> A farmer went out to sow his seed. As he was scattering the seed, some fell along the path, and the birds came and ate it up. Some fell on rocky places, where it did not have much soil. It sprang up quickly, because the soil was shallow. But when the sun came up, the plants were scorched, and they withered because they had no root. Other seed fell among thorns, which grew up and choked the plants. Still other seed fell on good soil, where it produced a crop—a hundred, sixty or thirty times what was sown.
> —MATTHEW 13:3–8

The soil of the heart reflects how we react to the Word of the Lord. The soils are all different, just as we are all different. What kept the seed from taking solid root was the poor condition of the soil. Similarly, what keeps us from letting Christ take hold of our life is the condition of our hearts and minds.

Sometimes our hearts are filled with hard ground or rocky places. Maybe a family member said something that made you callous. Maybe you don't feel accepted in society, so you don't want to accept anyone else. Maybe you had a negative experience with a church that left you cynical. Any of these events create negative thoughts—vain imaginations—that keep our hearts locked up and unwilling to hear the Word of God.

Sometimes there are thorns in our lives. We let the cares and desires of this world interfere with the Word of God trying to grow in us. We doubt God because we want worldly goods, which we think we can obtain by our own power. We are anxious and fearful; we don't allow God to have a real relationship with us.

Even if we plant a garden in good soil and don't cultivate it, weeds grow. We can have Christ planted in our hearts, but we must be "cultivated" so that worldly imaginations don't destroy us. What happens with the positive imaginations, when the seed of God's Word lands in the good soil? Those seeds, His Word, change us. The imaginations of Christ begin to fill our minds. We praise Him so much and are so thankful to Him that the diamonds associated with the crown of His majesty pierce our hard soil—our hearts and minds.

If we expect any kind of soil to produce fruit, it needs to be plowed. In the same way, we need to break up the soil of our minds and let God sow His Word in it. The prophet, Jeremiah, directed the Israelites to do allow this change of heart:

> This is what the LORD says to the men of Judah and to Jerusalem: "Break up your unplowed ground and do not

sow among thorns. Circumcise yourselves to the LORD,
circumcise your hearts…"

—JEREMIAH 4:3–4

We cannot allow the soil of our hearts to be preoccupied with
the world. Our lives cannot be filled with positive imaginations
of Christ until we get rid of our earthly ways of thinking and are
reborn spiritually with Him.

We must search our hearts and pull out all the weeds the world
has sown—weeds of anger, bitterness, greed, and most of all,
selfishness. We need to let God take away all the hardness and
resentments of our hearts, becoming willing to forgive others.
And we must be abandoned to God—and to Him alone. Listen
to the prophet Hosea:

> Sow for yourselves righteousness, reap the fruit of unfail-
> ing love, and break up your unplowed ground; for it is
> time to seek the LORD.
>
> —HOSEA 10:12

Seeds do not always grow. Their fruitful development depends
on the soil. As humans, we have a choice about our development. It
is up to us to determine whether we are going to receive His Word,
His seed. When He touches our hearts, do we respond to Him with
complete surrender, seeking to fill our lives with His thoughts?

Remember, the imaginations of our minds are what we become.
Do we choose negative, earthly thoughts, or do we choose the
complete peace, joy, and thankfulness of the everlasting God?

CHAPTER 15

React or Respond?

When we give medicines to our patients, they either react to them or they respond to them. Reaction is bad. Response is good. This is a picture of the way we handle life's circumstances, whether good or bad. We can react in negative and harmful ways or we can respond in a godly way. Our sense of satisfaction determines whether we react or respond. Consider what happens when someone insults you. Do you react or respond? Listen to the following instruction:

> A gentle answer turns away wrath, but a harsh word stirs up anger.
>
> —PROVERBS 15:1

A gentle answer comes from positive imaginations, a loving attitude, thinking like Christ. A harsh word comes from negative imaginations, a worldview in which we put ourselves first and are quick to judge and condemn others. For example, when people invest in the stock market, they have imaginations of money. Those imaginations can be good or bad. They can imagine how they will use money to serve God and help others. Or they can imagine how successful they will be if they have more money. Then they quit thinking of God.

The complex life of King David is full of examples we can follow and lessons we can apply to our own lives. He demonstrated over and over again the rich blessings of godly imaginations and the pain and destruction caused by worldly thoughts. David was a very special person to God. "I have found David son of Jesse a man after my own heart," God said of him (Acts 13:22).

As a boy, David was anointed to be king of Israel. As king, he was a mighty military commander and powerful leader. He accomplished great deeds in the name of the Lord; he returned the Ark of the Covenant to the people of Israel. He was a person of action, an author of beautiful poetry, a loyal friend, and a judicious ruler and leader.

God loved David so much that He made a covenant with him:

> Your house and your kingdom will endure forever before me; your throne will be established forever.
>
> —2 SAMUEL 7:16

God honored David by pledging that Jesus Christ, the Messiah, would be his descendant. From the house and family of David would come the Savior of the world. But David also had some grievous failings. He sinned greatly before the Lord and he repented deeply. His life shows us that no one lives in perfect obedience to the law. It also shows us how much God desires a relationship with each of us.

Two incidents in David's life will reveal to us how thoughts affect actions and change our lives. The first happened early in David's life. The Israelites were at war with the Philistines. David's older brothers went off to battle, while David, who was still a boy, stayed home to look after the family's sheep. David's father, Jesse, sent David to the battlefield with provisions for his brothers and other troops. When he reached the Israelite camp, he had his first encounter with Goliath, the warrior-giant. He heard Goliath taunt the Israelites, and he saw the Israelites cower before him.

David was outraged that Goliath could insult the people of God in such a way. And he was equally outraged that the "armies of the living God" would run (1 Samuel 17:26). The army of Israel had imaginations of fear and doubt. David would not be influenced by such thinking. His faith would not be shaken, even by a nine-foot tall warrior-giant. David made his way to Saul, the king and commander of Israel. "Let no one lose heart on account of this Philistine; your servant will go and fight him" (1 Samuel 17:32).

To Saul, this was unthinkable. David was a boy; Goliath a seasoned soldier. But David knew he had one additional factor in his favor: faith in God. He knew the God who kept him safe as he defended sheep from lions and bears would keep him safe in battle against Goliath. So convincing was his declaration of faith that Saul agreed to let David fight.

Goliath was insulted that the Israelites would send an inexperienced boy into battle against him. David saw Goliath, with all his impressive armor, shield, and sword. His courage didn't waver. He didn't run. His trust in God was unshakable. He had faith in God's promises:

> You come against me with sword and spear and javelin, but I come against you in the name of the LORD Almighty, the God of the armies of Israel, whom you have defied. This day the LORD will hand you over to me, and I'll strike you down and cut off your head...and the whole world will know that there is a God in Israel. All those gathered here will know that it is not by sword or spear that the LORD saves; for the battle is the LORD's, and he will give all of you into our hands.
>
> —1 SAMUEL 17:45–47

David knew that mere weapons were no match for the Almighty God. His thoughts were focused on the power of God; no earthly show of strength could weaken his faith.

> So David triumphed over the Philistine with a sling and a stone; without a sword in his hand he struck down the Philistine and killed him.
>
> —1 SAMUEL 17:50

David's imaginations of faith guided his actions. He believed God would protect him and give him the victory. So he felt bold in battle.

His encounter was one of courage because he trusted in God.

The second incident happened years later, after David had become a mighty king. Unhappily, we encounter another kind of imagination in David in this situation. The Book of Second Samuel tells us about David's great struggle with sin.

In one of Israel's military campaigns, David stayed in Jerusalem while sending the troops off to war. Late one night, he saw a beautiful woman bathing and found out she was Bathsheba, wife of Uriah.

Already, David was in trouble. He wasn't with his troops, leading his army in battle for the Lord. He was neglecting his business and therefore was more susceptible to temptation. And even though he knew Bathsheba was married, that fact didn't keep him from acting on his ungodly imaginations.

> Then David sent messengers to get her. She came to him, and he slept with her.
>
> —2 SAMUEL 11:4

David fell further and further into a web of sin and deceit. When Bathsheba discovered she was pregnant, David sent for her husband, allowing him the opportunity to go home, hoping to trick everyone into thinking that Uriah was the baby's father. That didn't' work. So noble was Uriah that he refused to have pleasure with his wife while his troops were far away in battle. Unlike David, he focused his imaginations on the task at hand: success in battle. So David hatched another plan.

> In the morning David wrote a letter to Joab and sent it with Uriah. In it he wrote, "Put Uriah in the front line where the fighting is fiercest. Then withdraw from him so he will be struck down and die."
>
> —2 SAMUEL 11:14–15

First he committed adultery, then murder. After Uriah's death, David married Bathsheba, but the matter didn't end there. God knew the truth. In an encounter with the prophet Nathan, David finally understood the deep sorrow he had brought upon God and the pain he had brought to everyone involved in the deception.

> Then David said to Nathan, "I have sinned against the LORD." Nathan replied, "The Lord has taken away your sin. You are not going to die. But because by doing this you have made the enemies of the LORD show utter contempt, the son born to you will die."
>
> —2 SAMUEL 12:13–14

David had let a mind-set of selfishness, greed, and lust influence his actions. As king, he had everything he could ever want, yet he still wanted something more—Bathsheba. He was no longer satisfied in the promises of God. In his selfishness, he lost his mind-set of faith in God, and he brought about pain, suffering, and death. The child did indeed die. But when David deeply repented (see Psalm 51), God forgave David. And He blessed David and Bathsheba with another son, Solomon, who became one of the wisest men of the Bible.

These two incidents show how David's actions were influenced by his affections and his imaginations. When he looked to God, he succeeded; when he looked inward, at his own selfish desires, he failed.

What do we learn from David's experiences? In our decisions and our actions, our mind-set is critical. Now, we may not face physical giants such as Goliath in our daily lives. But we do face choices every day about how we focus our minds and how we act.

Few of us will destroy kingdoms because of our thoughts, but families and friends can suffer because of the actions that result from vain imaginations. The meditations and imaginations of our minds determine our actions. Shall we become as noble kings for the Lord or shall we shamefully disrupt our lives because of vain imaginations? The New Testament warns us:

> Those who live according to the sinful nature have their minds set on what that nature desires; but those who live in accordance with the Spirit have their minds set on what the Spirit desires…the mind controlled by the Spirit is life and peace.
>
> —ROMANS 8:5–6

In this passage, the apostle Paul tells us to focus on Christ. And when we think on Him, we will respond to life's circumstances with godly imaginations. May His peace and love guide our actions in every situation. Amen!

CHAPTER 16

The Battle

Like David, we are under attack every day by worldly imaginations. Why do we imagine ourselves doing things that are wrong rather than imagine ourselves praying? Why do we seek after material possessions rather than being with our families, serving God, sharing the Gospel? Why can't we keep our thoughts focused on the Lord?

A man I know runs a help-line for young people in distress. He said the biggest problem faced by people seeking his help is the constant warring between worldly goals and godly ones. All of us are under assault. We are constantly barraged by the goals of the world. The world says it is OK to focus on ourselves first, it is OK to acquire more goods and possessions, it is OK to cheat, steal, and lie if it helps us get what we want. This message is repeated every day by television, the Internet, Madison Avenue advertising, and sometimes even by friends and family.

Under such an assault, even the strongest of us can succumb to worldly imaginations. It makes sense that if we play in a garbage pile, we are going to get dirty. If we allow garbage—worldly thoughts and vain imaginations—to fill our minds, we will become worldly. Earthly desires are harmful; they destroy us and those around us. But we cannot give up when our thoughts are under attack. We cannot let worldly thoughts win. This is not a minor skirmish that we can ignore. Those who let the world win are headed for eternity without Christ! Consider this wisdom:

> When tempted, no one should say, "God is tempting me." For God cannot be tempted by evil, nor does he tempt anyone; but each one is tempted when, by his own evil desire, he is dragged away and enticed. Then, after desire has conceived, it gives birth to sin; and sin, when it is full-grown, gives birth to death.
>
> —James 1:13–15

The Scriptures describe a battle for our eternal life that pits us against the full force of Satan:

> For our struggle is not against flesh and blood, but against the rulers, against the authorities, against the powers of this dark world and against the spiritual forces of evil in the heavenly realms.
>
> —Ephesians 6:12

Why would Satan care what kinds of thoughts fill our mind? Why does he continually tempt us? Because he knows that *we are what we think*. This battle for the mind is the most important fight of our lives because the choices we make, influenced by our thoughts and imaginations, determine our eternal destiny. Who will we let win this life and death struggle—Satan or the Almighty God?

Our goal is to think as God thinks, not to be controlled by worldly attitudes. If we think about the world, we are going to be disappointed. If we think about God, we are going to be truly rewarded—now and for eternity. Yet, according to the Scriptures, people's minds can be blinded by Satan's lies:

> The god of this age has blinded the minds of unbelievers, so that they cannot see the light of the gospel of the glory of Christ, who is the image of God.
>
> —2 Corinthians 4:4

Satan comes through many conduits and channels. He may be dressed well, culturally accepted, and advertised beautifully, but he is still Satan. He will attack each of us differently, because he knows our individual weaknesses. But he seeks the same result in each of us: He wants to blind us to the glory of Christ. He lures us away from the person of Jesus Christ gently at first, but before long we are tied up in his bonds of deception. Satan can convince us to doubt God as he did Adam and Eve, saying in essence, *Can you really believe God and what He says?* (See Genesis 3:1.)

As Satan lured Adam and Eve, he can do the same with us today and will continue to do it tomorrow! It is difficult to avoid. We have to battle our own human nature as well as the lies of Satan. Worldly thoughts can easily yank at us, seducing us: "Come on, let's go have a good time." What we are really headed for is trouble. When our desires take us away from faith in God's promises, they become sin.

At times, all of us have used our imaginations in hurtful, self-ish ways. We face a constant battle between the thoughts and desires of this world and the faith that leads to surrender to God and a transforming relationship with Christ.

All sins—all negative attitudes and harmful actions—originate in us when we are lacking that transforming faith, not believing in the promises of God and allowing our selfishness to take control of our thoughts and actions. The Bible teaches that everything that does not come from faith is sin. (See Romans 14:23.) Anything that is not an expression of faith in the person of Jesus Christ is sin. Anything that is not of faith will lead to an aberration of peace, an aberration of joy, and an aberration of love.

Sin is not ultimately against other people; it is against God. Sin is preferring the world to God. Sin is when we are not satisfied with God; we need the world to satisfy us. Such behavior is the outgrowth of a deceitful heart, a heart not truly focused on the pure and perfect imaginations of God. Jesus affirmed this fact:

> For out of the heart come evil thoughts, murder, adultery, sexual immorality, theft, false testimony, slander.
> —MATTHEW 15:19

The foundation for godly living is godly thinking. It is simple in concept, but it is not easy to perform. We must guard against dwelling on the "maybe" of temptations. For example, maybe we are attracted to someone with whom we have a close friendship. And if the relationship isn't going right with a spouse, this other person seems even more attractive. Then we think about what "maybe" could happen.

We need to defeat these "maybes" with an emphatic "NO." We must bring these imaginations under control before they take on "a life of their own." We should focus on seeking the Lord's face and His help to overcome and bring all these thoughts captive.

Fighting sin and fighting Satan is a continual process. Think about it as taking care of a yard. We can go out every day and pull the weeds out of our yard. But if we don't pull all the root system, the weeds keep growing back. So we get a gardening tool to dig out all the roots and some weed killer to make sure we stop them from growing back.

And after a while, sure enough, the weeds are gone. But then we discover that moles are burrowing underneath the yard. Now we have to find a way to destroy the moles. That is how sin works in our lives. We have to forcefully destroy it and constantly attack it.

But we also have to make sure we replace the "weeds" with something else in our lives to keep Satan away. We must let God's Holy Spirit and His Word fill our lives. We must let our imaginations of loving and serving God and others stir up holy desires and efforts. Otherwise selfish, sinful imaginations will continue to take root in our lives and produce destructive thoughts and actions.

We have talked before about the need to surrender our selfishness and our pride. Paul uses strong language to warn us about the dangers of selfish desires and vain imaginations. He also tells us how to battle sin—finding satisfaction in the promises of God:

> If anyone teaches false doctrines and does not agree to the sound instruction of our Lord Jesus Christ and to godly teaching, he is conceited and understands nothing.

He has an unhealthy interest in controversies and quarrels about words that result in envy, strife, malicious talk, evil suspicions and constant friction between men of corrupt mind, who have been robbed of the truth and who think that godliness is a means to financial gain.

But godliness with contentment is great gain. For we brought nothing into the world, and we can take nothing out of it. But if we have food and clothing, we will be content with that. People who want to get rich fall into temptation and a trap and into many foolish and harmful desires that plunge men into ruin and destruction. For the love of money is a root of all kinds of evil. Some people, eager for money, have wandered from the faith and pierced themselves with many griefs.

—1 Timothy 6:3–10

Remember the story of Samson? He was totally committed to God for awhile, but then he started looking for worldly satisfaction. We can be like Samson, falling victim to sin when our earthly appetites lead us away from satisfaction in the Lord. We can succumb to the "Delilahs of the mind" because we aren't satisfied in our current circumstances. And like Samson, we can turn from our sin, call upon the Lord, and trust in Him for our strength. He will restore us when we seek His forgiveness.

What is our Delilah? There are many "faces" of Delilah that tempt people with desire. We are covetous by nature. We want more and more. Advertising agencies tap into this desire, increasing the aroma of covetousness by suggesting we need bigger and better possessions. Coveting, whether in the form of money, lust, careers, or other idols of the world, draws us off the path of believing in the promises of God. It makes us believe we can be content with external possessions and goals. There is no lasting meaning in the idols of the world.

Some people struggle with the "Delilah" of being content with their material status in life. They can never have enough material possessions, no matter how much they own. They are lured by the false imagination that material goods offer complete comfort. They need to consider this wisdom:

> Whoever loves money never has money enough; whoever loves wealth is never satisfied with his income. This too is meaningless. As goods increase, so do those who consume them. And what benefit are they to the owner except to feast his eyes on them?
> —ECCLESIASTES 5:10–11

I know people who battle the "Delilah" of desire for more money—the tangible measure of success in this world—to bring them contentment. J. P. Morgan was once asked, "How much money does it take to make people who work for you happy?" He said, "Oh, just a little bit more than they have."

Who of us has not wanted just a little more? Money is one of the greatest lures into false thinking—wanting man's power, not the power of the Almighty God. The desire to be rich, to buy human accomplishments, is a snare and a trap. It takes our focus off God's promise that He will provide. We do not see the danger until we are in it. Greed is a deadly vice. It kills and blots out God's presence within us.

> For the love of money is a root of all kinds of evil. Some people, eager for money, have wandered from the faith and pierced themselves with many griefs.
> —1 TIMOTHY 6:10

True spiritual wealth is an attitude. The love of money is the sin, not money itself. The richest person is the one who can say: *I don't need anything more. I have a relationship with the living God.*

For some, their "Delilah" is not material possessions or money, but a career or place of employment. They may never be content in a job, and therefore move from job to job. And some let their desire for success at work interfere with their performance, their relationships with co-workers and, most of all, with their desire to do work that honors and glorifies God first.

> Therefore, my dear brothers, stand firm. Let nothing move you. Always give yourselves fully to the work of the Lord, because you know that your labor in the Lord is not in vain.
>
> —1 CORINTHIANS 15:58

Our work needs to reflect our focus on God. We especially need to stand firm in the workplace, serving God and loving others.

For some, it is the arena of personal relationships that poses a range of problems. I have seen marriages in which one spouse is seeking a "perfect" partner and therefore is never content. So that person strays from the marriage to seek perfection and ends up destroying the relationship. We have to let imaginations of God transform us into people who are content in relationships with others. Each spouse is "the best significant other" when the other is satisfied with him or her, and him or her alone.

Jesus gives us the formula for the right relationships.

> ""Love the Lord your God with all your heart and with all your soul and with all your mind.' This is the first and greatest commandment. And the second is like it: 'Love your neighbor as yourself.'"
>
> —MATTHEW 22:37–39

Some face the "Delilah" represented by the need for recognition from others. The Lord expects us to be content in relationship with Him, not seeking awards and glory and praise from others. Striving for self-attained recognition takes us away from seeking the mind of Christ. When we seek to get our recognition from the world, we usually fail to get enough. We think we don't get the recognition we deserve. Or even if we get what we deserve, we still want more. Instead, what we should seek is to be aligned with Christ, allowing ourselves to be fulfilled by His love. His standard, not the praise of men, is what matters.

> For it is not the one who commends himself who is approved, but the one whom the Lord commends.
> —2 CORINTHIANS 10:18

Some people crave excitement and adventure and will make reckless decisions based on their adventurous desires. I know doctors who make decisions in their profession just to create excitement. I know people who choose their business projects for the excitement the project generates. These choices are not always beneficial in helping or serving others. The desire for excitement and adventure must be balanced with the desire to serve God. We find genuine excitement and adventure in our relationship with Him. With David, we can declare:

> The LORD is my strength and my shield; my heart trusts in him, and I am helped. My heart leaps for joy and I will give thanks to him in song.
> —PSALM 28:7

Our thoughts determine our destiny, as we have discussed. God knows this. Satan knows this. Do we act as though we know it? Why do we choose to be half-filled by the material goods and other "Delilahs" of this world rather than completely filled, and completely content, with the Lord God? Like a child without goals, we idle away our time in recreation, in ambition for our careers, in social activities and functions, in half-hearted relationships. Our minds become filled with how we are going to fit everything in, and God gets squeezed into a corner of fleeting acknowledgment. How many times have we wanted money and the pleasures it pretends to buy, only to later regret that we have lost sight of God?

We damage ourselves and our relationship with Him when we chase our "Delilahs." Life in this world is full of tinsel, of fleeting diversions and thrills and entertainments that lure us away from

God. And even though we may lose our focus on Him, we still feel the need to be content. So we seek satisfaction in various escapes—mystic escapes, moral escapes, or material escapes.

Here is an often-told story to illustrate this search. A certain man grew up on a farm in a small town. He worked and plowed on this farm. But while he was on the farm he dreamed of one day searching the world, looking for diamonds. To him, diamonds were the greatest symbol of riches, beauty, and success in life. When he woke up in the morning, he thought of diamonds. When he plowed a field, he thought of mining for diamonds. When he went to bed at night, he had dreams of diamonds.

Eventually, he sold his farm, left his hometown, and went out into the world. For forty years he hunted around the globe for diamonds. He became an explorer and negotiator so he could start diamond mines in many obscure places. He became an inventor so he could devise new mining techniques. He became a scientist so he could determine the best places to search for diamonds. But he never reached his goal. He never uncovered diamonds.

He finally went back to his hometown. He was a broken man who was ready to spend his remaining years of life where he had started. But he had to reintroduce himself to the townspeople because he had changed so much during the years of searching for diamonds.

Upon his return he learned that the largest diamond ever mined was found on the farm he had once owned. He had sold the land for a pittance, and now it was worth a fortune. His search for success had taken him around the world, and the one thing he had truly wanted had been under his nose on his own farm.

His search had been misdirected. In looking for earthly success, he found only disappointment. If he had been content, appreciating what God had given him, certainly he would have found earthly success, because the diamond was in his land the whole time. But he would have also found a richer satisfaction through the person of Jesus Christ.

How about us? Are we aware of the battle for our minds? Do

we acknowledge the temptations of this world? Are we ready to fight worldly thoughts and surrender ourselves to God? Do we have a worldly view or an eternal perspective?

> Do not love the world or anything in the world. If anyone loves the world, the love of the Father is not in him. For everything in the world—the cravings of sinful man, the lust of his eyes and the boasting of what he has and does—comes not from the Father but from the world. The world and its desires pass away, but the man who does the will of God lives forever.
>
> —1 JOHN 2:15–17

With faith in God, nothing can defeat us! We are walking in God and He is in us. We have His love, His power, His peace. We trust in His eternal provision. We can rest in His presence now and for eternity.

So often we know this in our hearts, but our minds war against it, creating confusion, distortion, and anxiety. For example, we can have faith in our hearts, but our minds become afraid. So we worry, we let ourselves be intimidated and lured by the attitudes and material goods of this world. We find ourselves in sinful attitudes—the breeding ground for selfishness and vain imaginations.

The god of this world has a plan to catch and snare those who have great potential in the kingdom of God. Will we be lured away by the lies of this god? Or will we let our minds be satisfied with the promises of God?

> You were taught, with regard to your former way of life, to put off your old self, which is being corrupted by its deceitful desires; to be made new in the attitude of your minds; and to put on the new self, created to be like God in true righteousness and holiness.
>
> —EPHESIANS 4:22–24

We need to put on the new attitude of thanksgiving and worship. Then we will see eternity stretching out before us with the person of Jesus Christ. Let us look no longer to the world for solutions and fulfillment; let us look to Christ. We will be engulfed in His presence forever! He will be our provider forever!

Chapter 17

Making Our Choice

At age sixteen, our physical appearance is largely determined by what we have been given through heredity. By age sixty, our looks are determined more by the lifestyle choices we have made. We really do choose most of the elements that effect our life. We can choose to exercise and eat right or we can choose to be unconcerned about our diet and weight. We can choose to enjoy our work or to complain about it. We can choose to be generous or stingy; to criticize others or to encourage them. We can choose to be introverts or extroverts. We can choose happiness or sorrow.

Life is full of choices. The greatest choice of all is choosing what we will think. We choose how we control our minds. We are responsible for what we think and what we do with our thoughts. And we are responsible for the results of our thoughts. When we decide what we will allow to motivate us, we decide what kind of people we will be.

We choose whether to be positive or negative, angry, violent, depressed, or worried. We choose to either be constructive, using emotions that build us up, or to be negative, using emotions that damage us and those around us. We choose to be satisfied in God's promises or to be selfish, filled with worldly desires.

Most importantly, we choose either eternal life with Jesus Christ or eternity without Him based on choosing to align ourselves to God in this life. When we choose God, we get our benefits, in Christian terms, as His blessings. It is up to us to choose spiritual death or life everlasting in Christ. In the battle for our eternal life, which side do we choose? Again, the New Testament warns:

You adulterous people, don't you know that friendship with the world is hatred toward God? Anyone who chooses to be a friend of the world becomes an enemy of God.

—JAMES 4:4

The greatest choice we face is whether we focus our thoughts on the world or on God? Do we fix our minds on Him? Or do we clutter our minds with false imaginations? Do we direct our thoughts according to worldly standards or do we seek the mind of Christ? The Old Testament prophet, Elijah, confronted King Ahab and the people of Israel about this choice.

King Ahab was one of the worst kings of Israel. The book of 1 Kings describes how Ahab set up the worship of Baal, a mock deity. His wife, Queen Jezebel, worshiped idols, practiced witchcraft, and was a malicious, vicious woman. Elijah, the great prophet, told the Israelites that God was displeased with them because they worshiped idols. He warned them that a drought would cover the land and punish them for their sins. Then God told Elijah to leave the region and directed the prophet to a safe place where God would provide for him. The Israelites, under the reign of Ahab, were on their own.

Sure enough, the drought came and famine was severe. Queen Jezebel persecuted the followers of God, killing many and forcing the remainder to go into hiding. Finally, God ordered Elijah to return to the region. "Go and present yourself to Ahab, and I will send rain on the land" (1 Kings 18:1).

Elijah confronted Ahab and told him to "summon the people from all over Israel to meet me on Mount Carmel. And bring the four hundred and fifty prophets of Baal and the four hundred prophets of Asherah, who eat at Jezebel's table" (1 Kings 18:19).

Ahab and the people gathered, expecting Elijah to bless them and pray for rain; but Elijah had other priorities:

> Elijah went before the people and said, "How long will you waver between two opinions? If the LORD is God, follow him; but if Baal is God, follow him." But the people said nothing.
>
> —1 KINGS 18:21

The people were silent. They refused to take a stand about whom they would follow and how they would direct their thoughts. To this point, some had worshiped the Lord God and some had worshiped Baal. Even worse, sometimes they worshiped one and sometimes the other. Elijah knew that those who waver in their loyalty are not only unstable in their faith, they do not function well in the rest of their lives.

Elijah proposed a test. Each side would prepare a sacrifice and call on the name of its God (god) to light the fire around the sacrifice. The supporters of Baal had all the external advantages. Their camp included 450 prophets and the power of the king and his court. Elijah was just one man, alone in his faith in the Lord. The people agreed to the contest.

From morning to evening, the prophets of Baal called on their god. They danced, they shouted, they even cut themselves with swords to draw blood, trying to appease Baal. Nothing happened. "There was no response, no one answered, no one paid attention" (1 Kings 18:29).

Then it was Elijah's turn. He built an altar with twelve stones, one for each tribe of Israel. He placed the wood around the altar and prepared the sacrifice. Then he did something amazing. He soaked the offering and the wood with water. Three times. There was no way on earth that the wood would catch fire.

> At the time of sacrifice, the prophet Elijah stepped forward and prayed: "O LORD, God of Abraham, Isaac and Israel, let it be known today that you are God in Israel and that I am your servant and have done all these things at your command. Answer me, O LORD, answer me, so these people will know that you, O LORD, are

God, and that you are turning their hearts back again."

Then the fire of the Lord fell and burned up the sacrifice, the wood, the stones and the soil, and also licked up the water in the trench.

When all the people saw this, they fell prostrate and cried, "The Lord—he is God! The Lord—he is God!"

—1 KINGS 18:36-39

After such a powerful display, the people chose to worship the true God. Today, we are faced with the same choice. Do we choose the fleeting pleasures that come from worshiping false gods? Or do we choose the living God, the mighty Jehovah who sends fire from heaven to show His power and might? Jesus describes our situation this way:

No one can serve two masters. Either he will hate the one and love the other, or he will be devoted to the one and despise the other.

—MATTHEW 6:24

We must be willing to become spiritual warriors as we come to Christ. When we choose the eternal life of God, we choose sides. Even though we may still be assaulted by the thoughts of this world, we must choose to stay focused on God.

So much of life tries to knock us down, knock us out of the ring, and knock us out of the fight. We must choose whether we get back up and keep going. Every day when we wake up we choose whether to love and serve God. We choose whether our imaginations of Him are positive, or whether we are going to fail that day because of negative imaginations and thoughts. Every day matters. Every day makes a difference.

Bill Anderson, a former pastor in Clearwater, Florida, and I talk about how so many elements in life compete for our attention. Each one seems important. As a pastor, Bill has seen many people wrestle with the decision to choose Jesus Christ. He has seen them struggle to keep their minds and hearts focused on

God. Sometimes we think we can have it all. We think we do not have to choose between God and the world. So we play along to get along.

In reality, living this kind of unfocused life consists of being filled with great anxiety, stress, and frustration. Lacking the ability to concentrate on our work and to follow through on promises and commitments, we become inconsistent, indifferent, and incompetent in all we try to accomplish. Being divided between the two is like having one foot in one boat and the other foot in another boat. We will be jerked apart and end up drowning.

God wants our total commitment—all of us or none of us. He doesn't want some attention from us when it is convenient, or only when we are in trouble. There is but one God, and He will meet our needs.

We will not choose imaginations focused on Christ if we have a worldly perspective. Leonardo da Vinci said, "Perspective is to art what a bridle is to a horse or a rudder to a boat." What is our perspective? What is our rudder? What guides us? An eternal perspective will give us the ability to know where to go and how to control ourselves. Let us have an imagination of anticipation: eternal life with Christ—an eternal life that begins the minute we surrender to Him, the minute we commit ourselves to Him in faith, the minute we accept His priceless grace.

We are freed from all the concerns of the world, the affections of the world. We are not merely reformed, trying to improve what already is within us. Instead we are transformed. God has given us a glorious eternal life that we can enjoy this day, this moment.

Let us imagine that eternal city, where there is perfect peace and complete joy, where we are in harmony with God and others. We have no worries, we have no fears. We have eternal life with our Creator, Redeemer, and Sustainer. Richard Baxter, in his book, *The Saints' Everlasting Rest*, exhorts us to take a walk in the New Jerusalem every day and enjoy the place Christ is preparing for us.[1]

Let us imagine that city every day. May that vision guide us every day, so that our eternal life with Christ begins now. Then the focus of our imaginations is to always be "with Him," fully focused on the mind of Christ every day.

Have you made the choice about whom you will follow? Have you decided what will motivate your thoughts? Have you decided what kind of person you will be? If not, let me encourage you to make the most important choice in life—that choice for Jesus Christ! Discover the eternal fountains of joy and peace, thanksgiving and hope, love and grace that He holds for you and for me. Jesus calls each of us to come to His cross and find forgiveness, and then to follow Him. I pray you hear His voice today.

CHAPTER 18

Spiritual Conditioning

Once we have been quickened by the Holy Spirit, can we sit back and relax? Is our life going to be a perfect example of satisfaction and peace? Is there anything more we need to do?

We have the mind of Jesus because we are being transformed by the Word and the Holy Spirit. However, we must refocus every day. We must reprogram our minds so that we become strong Christians. The secret to keeping the true imaginations of God constantly in our hearts is to daily reapply our minds to our relationship with Him, as the Scriptures teach:

> Therefore, prepare your minds for action.
> —1 PETER 1:13

> Be self-controlled and alert. Your enemy the devil prowls around like a roaring lion looking for someone to devour.
> —1 PETER 5:8

In sports, training makes an athlete stronger. If we are committed to a sport, we train for it and receive rewards for our performance. If we are committed to our profession, we get our rewards from it. If we are committed to the world, we get blessings from the world.

Spiritual conditioning is just as vital as physical training. We become "couch potatoes" spiritually unless we train our minds to focus on God. If we are committed to Him, we get our blessings from God's presence working through us. As we choose to train our minds, the Scriptures show us how:

Let us fix our eyes on Jesus, the author and perfecter of our faith, who for the joy set before him endured the cross, scorning its shame, and sat down at the right hand of the throne of God.

—HEBREWS 12:2

We need to fix our eyes on Jesus. As an athlete conditions his body, so we must condition all the elements of our minds—our daydreams and fantasies, expectations, attitudes, thoughts, meditations, images, vision—to find satisfaction in God's promises. The only way to control those imaginations is to think of God in everything we do. We must be with Him and enjoy Him in everything!

We need to think of Christ not only as the Savior who saved us once through repentance, but we must think of Him as continually saving us as we constantly wash our minds and wash our thoughts. We must live in a state of constantly asking God to forgive our rebellious nature and warring against it ourselves:

We demolish arguments and every pretension that sets itself up against the knowledge of God, and we take captive every thought to make it obedient to Christ.

—2 CORINTHIANS 10:5

With all our might, we have to take our thoughts captive and diligently seek the transformation of our minds by the power of the Holy Spirit. (See Galatians 5:16.) We should seek for His thoughts to become our thoughts, His will to become our wills and His heart to become our hearts.

To build a fortress, the builder places one brick at a time. Few things are accomplished immediately. In our physical development, our mental development, our athletic development, and our spiritual development, we must take one area and grow a little bit each day.

All of us are responsible for our thoughts, whether they are based in the mind of Christ or directed by the desires of this world. Since God has given us the responsibility for our thoughts, He has given us the tools to control and direct them. We are responsible for the choices we make about how we act on our thoughts.

We cannot afford to be spiritual "couch potatoes." We must develop thought processes that focus on God and our relationship with Him in His eternal kingdom. Then our actions will be based on our eternal imaginations of Him, not on the false promises of this world. According to the Scriptures, it is imperative that we live consciously considering the effects of our thoughts:

> Above all else, guard your heart, for it is the wellspring of life.
>
> —PROVERBS 4:23

This verse reminds us that we are responsible for our imaginations, which affect all areas of our lives. Our imaginations are the spring from which all the issues and actions of our lives flow. It is essential that we guard our thoughts, keeping faithful, fervent, and focused on the Word of God. Our success is based not on a situation, but on our disposition. Our responses can never be based on outward circumstances, but on our inner attitudes and how well we condition our minds.

Let's look at some of the tools we can use to condition our minds, such as Bible study and prayer, discipline, and setting priorities.

THINK FIRST OR ACT FIRST?

If we control our thoughts, can we think ourselves into acting as Christ would? Or is the converse true? Do our Christlike actions help us take on the mind of Christ?

Many people would say it is certainly easier to act ourselves into godly thoughts, because the exercises of godly actions build up the muscles of godly thought. We act ourselves into our mindset. C. S. Lewis said that people turn into what they try to be. So, if we put our efforts into being full of joy, we become joyful.

There is a story told about a prince who was courting a woman. He was not very good looking, so he wore a mask of a handsome man to try to win the affections of the woman. And when he finally took off the mask he was truly handsome. Like that mask, our actions can mold our feelings.

We must create the action of walking out in faith, walking out in love. The action will create the feeling and we will become very much like the roles we play. We do it in sports, we do it in our professions, and we do it in relationships.

The great baseball pitcher, Nolan Ryan, once reportedly said that a person cannot control his mind until he controls his body. I think he was saying that we must be disciplined and balanced in all areas. It is important that we control not only our bodies, but more importantly our minds and our thoughts. Whether thoughts or actions come first is not the main issue; it is essential that the two be balanced.

We can get pulled into a mind-set, for example, that when we attend church, our actions are more important than our thoughts and attitudes. We can start to believe that if we give enough money to a church, or join enough committees, or do enough work in the name of the church, that our actions are sufficient. In other words, we start to believe we find salvation in the church, not in the person of Jesus Christ.

We have to guard against letting religion and tradition take the place of Jesus. The goal is not to do things for God, but to be with Him. We should be people who accept His teachings, integrate ourselves with Him through His Word, His fellowship, and His people, caring for others through His love.

External change, changing our actions, is good. But it is not enough. We need to change our orientation. We must be focused on God. Our roots must be fed by His Word and nourished by the Holy Spirit. A tree, for example, takes years to develop deep roots and produce rich fruit. Christian maturity comes when our roots go deep into the soil of faith and the Word and our thoughts and imaginations are directed continually toward Him. Then our trunks grow larger and our limbs grow higher and we produce an abundance of fruit. Obeying Christ's teachings helps us grow to maturity in our faith and actions. Productive obedience results from His grace and law at work in our life.

Probably one of the greatest examples of actions producing thoughts is revealed in the way each of us treats his or her spouse. When we do kind acts for a spouse, before long, kind thoughts will be revived.

DISCIPLINE

Discipline may be the secret to success in the world. I have observed many people who have a solid foundation of intelligence and natural ability. However, those who succeed are the ones who discipline themselves to build upon that foundation.

I have seen tremendous athletes succeed or fail according to their attitude toward their sport. If they are disciplined, they eat right and train regularly. They are successful because they built upon a solid foundation through discipline. But those who rely solely on their physical abilities eventually fail.

In all walks of life, self-discipline makes the difference between people who succeed and those who fail. But how does discipline apply to faith? Discipline takes what we know in our heads and hearts and applies it in our life choices. Discipline makes the difference between knowledge (what we know) and wisdom (how we live).

John Wesley had a tremendous amount of knowledge about God while he was at Oxford. But it was his faith that produced one of the greatest demonstrations of discipline the world has ever seen. His many books, his constant preaching, traveling, and caring and ministering for others, all required an enormous amount of discipline. This godly lifestyle flowed from his transforming experience of faith at Aldersgate.

When we are tempted with thoughts that are inconsistent with Kingdom principles, we must discipline our minds to move on to godly thoughts. We must discipline our minds to focus on good thoughts of eternal significance. We can't dwell on those thoughts that are not full of faith. No one else can control one's mind. We each have to take responsibility for our thoughts and train ourselves on guiding and implementing those thoughts.

We must have spiritual discipline to follow God's commands. Yet our obedience is not to be practiced out of a sense of duty. Our obedience should flow from the love we feel for Him and our desire to live in His promises:

> If you obey my commands, you will remain in my love, just as I have obeyed my Father's commands and remain in his love.
>
> —JOHN 15:10

We do what the Lord wants us to do because we love Him and have faith in His eternal promises. We find a greater satisfaction when our lives are aligned with the Lord's will. Now, we may or may not be successful by worldly standards. But we reap a greater harvest through our obedience. Our lives glorify God now and for eternity.

There will be times in our lives when we lose sight of God's promises. We may be distracted by the promises of this world. We may begin to doubt God's Word. Then our actions will reflect the imaginations that stem from those thoughts. And our world will come crashing down. We will find no peace, and no productivity in life, when we live without faith in God's eternal sovereignty.

We must build a strong foundation by turning the Word of God into experience and relationship. The key is letting our obedience to Him provide the discipline we need:

> We want each of you to show this same diligence to the very end, in order to make your hope sure. We do not want you to become lazy, but to imitate those who through faith and patience inherit what has been promised.
>
> —HEBREWS 6:11–12

We need to build and rebuild on His promises. We need to return to our foundation—a sense of satisfaction in the life He has given us through Jesus Christ. May the actions of our life demonstrate the spiritual discipline that comes from living out the promises of God!

SETTING PRIORITIES

Is your mind filled with imaginations that are profitable and good—God's information? It is easy for us to allow our minds to be cluttered with imaginations that are not really important and that prevent us from having abundant life in Christ. Here is a quick exercise to measure your progress. Write down all the things you think about in a day—or an hour. Then determine which are Christlike and which are not.

One of the biggest dangers we have as Christians in controlling our minds is letting ourselves get too busy—filling our life with clutter. D. L. Moody polished the shoes of visitors when his students would not. He showed that he was not too busy to act out his love for Christ by serving others.

Bill McCartney, the founder of Promise Keepers, is also a former football coach. He would be the first person to tell us how vital it is to have a focused, controlled mind. It works not only on the football field, but in every arena of life. Being focused is what enables us to take on the mind of Christ.

Distractions can take us away from the mind of Christ. Our mind can get cluttered with thoughts that preoccupy us and detract from our relationship with the living, transforming God. The Scriptures affirm this sad reality:

> But the worries of this life, the deceitfulness of wealth and the desires for other things come in and choke the word, making it unfruitful.
>
> —MARK 4:19

Focusing on anything other than Christ will keep us from thinking like Him, worshiping Him, praying to Him, and being with Him. Each of us has interests we are passionate about, activities we love and enjoy. They can benefit us or they can harm us depending on our mind-set and the priority we give these areas of our lives. But when we worship these interests, when we order our lives around them, they become idols. And we no longer are focused on Christ first.

As I mentioned earlier, I loved to play the stock market. And with the economic boom in the past few years, the stock market was like a very lucrative poker game for me. A lot of people around me also were keenly interested in this game. We read reports, researched companies, and followed business trends. We had computers galore as we watched the market's ups and downs. It was fun! But it also was distracting. It took time away from reading spiritual material and spending quiet time to cultivate my relationship with the Lord.

There is nothing intrinsically wrong with the stock market, and there is nothing wrong with the people who work hard with it. The market is wonderful in its proper place. But it cannot take the place of our spiritual priorities. We cannot allow anything, good or bad, to distract us from taking on the mind of Christ. Passionately, diligently, in every way possible, we should seek God. And God gives wonderful promises to those who do:

> You will seek me and find me when you seek me with all your heart.
> —JEREMIAH 29:13

We cannot do everything in life. We have to set priorities, otherwise our minds and lives become cluttered and unfocused. And the top priority is to focus on God, sharing our entire lives with Him and always living in His presence.

Distractions take many forms. We frequently overload on life's demands and then find it difficult to make time to be with God. I have done that in my life. Haven't we all? How do we know when something takes us from the mind of Christ? If it keeps us from growing in our relationship with Him. If it keeps us from worshiping Christ, from praying to Christ, from being with Christ. We need to have Christ as our priority, and then give balance to these other interests.

We have to release the distractions so we can focus on God. Our thought processes, our behavior, our activities must reflect that focus. There have been times in my life when I have had to eliminate other activities, which are pleasant and profitable, so I could choose pursuits that would allow me to think on Christ. Each of us has distractions that keep us from the essentials of Christ. We must avoid these so we can focus on the eternal view of Christ.

When we can rid ourselves of distractions, life becomes much simpler and more peaceful. We need to make life simple so we can become one with God. We need to do away with other interests, the other gods, the other idols, that take our focus off God. We do not simplify our lives for simplicity's sake. Rather, we simplify our lives so we can focus more fully on God. We will do well to pray:

"Lord, teach us to be with You and to enjoy You in everything we do."

MEDITATE ON GOD'S WORD

One of the people I have known who was the closest to the Lord was my grandmother. She memorized the whole New Testament. She was with Christ because she had taken on the mind of Christ through her memory work. Memorizing the Word of God helped develop in her a godly spirit. The Word of God within her made her radiate His presence.

Think of it like this. When we are in love with someone, we read every one of their love letters. We treasure them, we study them, we memorize them. Each word is precious because we are in love and the letters reveal more about the person we love.

It is the same way with God. His love letters to us are recorded in the Bible. When we are in love with Him, we study His Word, we read it with great passion. We hunger to hear more about Him and about how much He loves us.

However, if we are not in love with another person, we may let their letters stack up on the kitchen counter with other mail. How often do we do that with God's Word? Some people say they have tried to read the Bible, but it is too difficult to read. Or they have trouble finding time to read. Or it doesn't seem to give them what they need. Are these really excuses that we devise because we are not fully surrendered to Him? Sometimes we are still selfish and don't want to invest the time in reading His Word. Sometimes we are preoccupied with daily tasks and don't truly open our minds to what His Word can reveal.

To keep our minds focused on godly images, we must know God's Word. We need to constantly go over the Word to make our ways right. The Scriptures give clear instruction regarding our walk:

> How can a young man keep his way pure? By living according to your word.
> —Psalm 119:9

> Blessed is the man who does not walk in the counsel of the wicked or stand in the way of sinners or sit in the seat of mockers. But his delight is in the law of the Lord, and on his law he meditates day and night.
> —Psalm 1:1–2

As we meditate on the Lord and His Word, our minds are filled with Him and we have fellowship with Him that brings victory and joy to our everyday living. We must think deliberately according to the Word of God. God will answer our questions through the Bible. We should study God's Word so we can apply it to our lives and reason intelligently with it. Knowing the meaning of God's Word and growing in our ability to understand it will unlock spiritual meaning for us for our eternity.

God's grace through the power of the Word will change us. But we must let that grace lead us into following the Word of God, so we have a firm salvation and grow in the image of God. The Word is what makes us and cleanses us. Maturity comes from grace and the law, or God's Word, mingling in us. Then our imaginations of God become evident as we live according to His word.

We can become so obsessed with the desires of the flesh and this world that we barely have time to acknowledge the Lord. We watch television, attend sporting events, and find ourselves engrossed in our careers and our hobbies. If we do not look at God's Word and find our real imaginations coming from that Word, we are not fulfilling our jobs as Christians. We must read God's Word to make us His complete and adequate children, equipped for every good work and effective servants for Him, as the Scriptures teach:

> Do not let this Book of the Law depart from your mouth; meditate on it day and night, so that you may be careful to do everything written in it. Then you will be prosperous and successful. Have I not commanded you? Be strong and courageous. Do not be terrified; do not be discouraged, for the LORD your God will be with you wherever you go.
>
> —JOSHUA 1:8–9

We have to identify our hearts and our minds with Christ so we will prosper by living close to God. And we need to fix His Word firmly in our hearts and minds so it can truly guide us. We need to say with the psalmist:

> I have hidden your word in my heart that I might not sin against you.
>
> —PSALM 119:11

One of the ways I keep God's Word in my heart is to memorize Scripture. Here are some of my favorites:

Who shall separate us from the love of Christ? Shall trouble or hardship or persecution or famine or nakedness or danger or sword? As it is written: "For your sake we face death all day long; we are considered as sheep to be slaughtered." No, in all these things we are more than conquerors through him who loved us. For I am convinced that neither death nor life, neither angels nor demons, neither the present nor the future, nor any powers, neither height nor depth, nor anything else in all creation, will be able to separate us from the love of God that is in Christ Jesus our Lord.

—ROMANS 8:35–39

Do not conform any longer to the pattern of this world, but be transformed by the renewing of your mind. Then you will be able to test and approve what God's will is— his good, pleasing and perfect will.

—ROMANS 12:2

If I speak in the tongues of men and of angels, but have not love, I am only a resounding gong or a clanging cymbal. If I have the gift of prophecy and can fathom all mysteries and all knowledge, and if I have a faith that can move mountains, but have not love, I am nothing. If I give all I possess to the poor and surrender my body to the flames, but have not love, I gain nothing. Love is patient, love is kind. It does not envy, it does not boast, it is not proud. It is not rude, it is not self-seeking, it is not easily angered, it keeps no record of wrongs. Love does not delight in evil but rejoices with the truth. It always protects, always trusts, always hopes, always perseveres. Love never fails. But where there are prophecies, they will cease; where there are tongues, they will be stilled; where there is knowledge, it will pass away. For we know in part and we prophesy in part, but when perfection comes, the imperfect disappears. When I was a child, I talked like a child, I thought like a child, I reasoned like a child. When I became a man,

I put childish ways behind me. Now we see but a poor reflection as in a mirror; then we shall see face to face. Now I know in part; then I shall know fully, even as I am fully known. And now these three remain: faith, hope and love. But the greatest of these is love.

—1 CORINTHIANS 13:1–13

I have been crucified with Christ and I no longer live, but Christ lives in me. The life I live in the body, I live by faith in the Son of God, who loved me and gave himself for me.

—GALATIANS 2:20

So that Christ may dwell in your hearts through faith. And I pray that you, being rooted and established in love, may have power, together with all the saints, to grasp how wide and long and high and deep is the love of Christ, and to know this love that surpasses knowledge—that you may be filled to the measure of all the fullness of God.

—EPHESIANS 3:17–19

Be imitators of God, therefore, as dearly loved children.

—EPHESIANS 5:1

Put on the full armor of God so that you can take your stand against the devil's schemes.

—EPHESIANS 6:11

Rejoice in the Lord always. I will say it again: Rejoice! Let your gentleness be evident to all. The Lord is near. Do not be anxious about anything, but in everything, by prayer and petition, with thanksgiving, present your requests to God. And the peace of God, which transcends all understanding, will guard your hearts and your minds in Christ Jesus.

—PHILIPPIANS 4:4–7

What we memorize is what we utilize. It is important that we memorize the Word of God and utilize its truths. Scripture that is merely read and not memorized is probably not utilized in our life. It is very important that we memorize Scripture so that we are in the habit of applying it daily in our lives.

USING BIBLE IMAGERY

The Bible is full of images and symbols that we can use to guide our imaginations: God as our loving Father, as our Shepherd, as our sovereign Lord, as our gracious King. These images give us a fuller vision of God. They show us that we can always trust Him to provide for us, to love us, to forgive us, to heal us. Imaginations make faith invigorating, positive, and joyful.

A very familiar chapter of the Bible is Psalm 23. It is full of images that God has designed to fill our thoughts: the shepherd, the sheep, the green pastures, the still waters, the dark valley, the shepherd's crook pulling us back on the path, the anointing of our heads with oil.

God has given us all of these are pictures to fill our minds, to fill our imaginations, and to fill our hearts with faith. Here we see God's wisdom in the way the Bible is written, and how imaginations can help us live lives that honor God.

Our imaginations can cause us to be captivated with God. We want to embrace God. We know, in our heads and in our hearts, that His promises to us are real. These imaginations bring us a genuine sense of satisfaction and joy in the life that God has given us. And our actions are guided by our satisfied imaginations.

Are our imaginations fixed on God, so that we have a mental picture of contentment? Or do we lose sight of God's promises and seek contentment in the goals and activities of this world—jobs, possessions, relationships, athletics, and pastimes?

God's Word is an essential guide for our imaginations. We can use the examples of people in the Bible and apply the lessons they learned to our lives. We can even picture ourselves in the Scriptures, envisioning ourselves as these people.

For example, we can see ourselves as the leper coming to Jesus for healing. We can see ourselves as David, growing in faith and also struggling with deceit and death. We can see ourselves as Ruth, choosing the God of Israel as her all in all. Every person in the Bible is a part of us, and we can and should learn from their experiences.

These Bible characters show us, in positive and negative ways, how the foundation for godly living is godly thinking. They teach us that godly thinking stems from imaginations that are satisfied with God.

> Since, then, you have been raised with Christ, set your hearts on things above, where Christ is seated at the right hand of God. Set your minds on things above, not on earthly things.
>
> —COLOSSIANS 3:1–2

The apostle Paul tells us that we need to focus on God first. We need to be satisfied with all He has given us. We do not need to search for fulfillment in the material goods and goals of this world. We will find ultimate satisfaction only in the loving arms of our Father.

PRAY WITHOUT CEASING

> Do not be anxious about anything, but in everything, by prayer and petition, with thanksgiving, present your requests to God.
>
> —PHILIPPIANS 4:6

A woman who worked at St. Luke's Cataract & Laser Institute, Jean Skinner, seemed to be in a continuous state of prayer. Jean's total relinquishment to Christ made her different from others, and that had a pronounced effect on everyone around her. She ministered constantly to others and changed many lives in the community. She would lead people to the Lord daily.

Jean would wake up at 5 a.m. and, with her prayer partner, would pray for thirty-five minutes to an hour. They would pray for everyone, and the prayers would frequently be broken with laughter and joy.

Jean had a beautiful life, but it was not an easy one. When she was in her early thirties, she had divorced after an abusive marriage, and with no formal education or training, she had no way to support herself. When she had nothing else to hold on to, she turned to the Lord. She overcame those obstacles by the strength of Jesus Christ. She grew close to a strong biblical group that prayed fervently and believed the Word of the Lord, standing on it firmly. Their total reliance on the Word and the person of Jesus Christ permeated her life. And even though Jean attended several different churches over the next twenty years, she had a positive affect on all the families with whom she associated. Her total reliance on God made her different from others.

By the world's standards, Jean did not have anything. But as God sees it, she had everything. When she died at age fifty-seven from cancer, all of us who loved her knew that she had gained what she could not lose. Her funeral was a joyous occasion because we all knew she was wrapped up in glory with the one she always thought about, the one she always sought to know, the one she loved with her whole heart and mind.

Jean's life holds a lesson for all of us. It seems to be a pattern that when we lose everything, we gain Christ. We don't have anything to hold onto besides Him. My father said, "You won't really hold onto Christ until He becomes the only one you have to hold on to." It may be at one of the greatest points in our life—the greatest point of despair—that we seek Him.

We turn to Him in prayer. We unburden ourselves and surrender to Him. We talk, He listens. He talks, we listen. Prayer is an essential tool in conditioning our minds. How can we focus our thoughts on Him if we do not talk with Him and listen to His voice?

ACTS is an acronym for practical steps to help us get started with a regular relationship of prayer: Adoration, Confession, Thanksgiving, and Supplication. As we briefly discuss each of these helpful steps, I encourage you to use the acronym to help you remember to practice them each day.

ADORATION

We adore God—His sovereignty, His creation, His total control of the world, who He is. We fall in love with Him for His greatness. Adoration of the one we love and care for brings total joy. We can join with the psalmist and praise the one we love:

> Sing to God, O kingdoms of the earth, sing praise to the Lord, to him who rides the ancient skies above, who thunders with mighty voice. Proclaim the power of God, whose majesty is over Israel, whose power is in the skies. You are awesome, O God, in your sanctuary; the God of Israel gives power and strength to his people. Praise be to God!
>
> —PSALM 68:32–35

CONFESSION

God knows our sins. We know our sins. Confession is the vehicle for throwing away our sins, for casting off the burdens of our sin. We can tell the Lord about all the times we have failed Him in our thoughts and our actions. We certainly cannot be arrogant or proud before Him because we have sinned against Him.

Yet we also show that we love Him because we clear the air of those sins; we pledge to start anew. And He gives us this fresh start.

> If we confess our sins, he is faithful and just and will forgive us our sins and purify us from all unrighteousness.
>
> —1 JOHN 1:9

He wants us to have the positive attitude of loving Him, knowing that when we fail Him, we can confess our failings and He will still love us. This enables us to be free of guilt and not be depressed with the knowledge of wrongdoing.

THANKSGIVING

We are thankful to God for everything He is and will be, for everything He has done for us, and everything He will do. Thanksgiving changes us from cynical, critical, slothful people into energetic, enthusiastic, appreciative people. We are thankful we can come to Him in confession and receive His forgiveness. The Bible teaches us to give thanks:

> Give thanks in all circumstances, for this is God's will for you in Christ Jesus.
> —1 THESSALONIANS 5:18

SUPPLICATION

A simple definition for *supplication* from the original Greek, *deesis*, is "request" or "petition."[1] The apostle Paul admonishes believers to put on the whole armor of God, which includes:

> Praying always with all prayer and supplication in the Spirit, being watchful to this end with all perseverance and supplication for all the saints.
> —EPHESIANS 6:18, NKJV

It is important that we are in supplication to God at all times. Do we ask God for everything or do we try to do it ourselves? We need to ask Him for our very substance. We need to live in His Jireh—His provision. We need to let Him take care of all our interpersonal relationships. We need to constantly practice His presence through these four steps, not failing to make our requests known to Him continually.

> Do not be anxious about anything, but in everything, by prayer and petition, with thanksgiving, present your requests to God.
>
> —PHILIPPIANS 4:6

Adoration. Confession. Thanksgiving. Supplication. All these elements are essential in any relationship. They are critical to the love, communication, forgiveness, respect, friendship, and enjoyment found in relationships with others. And they are truly important when we are talking about relationship with our Lord.

Our adoration of Him is simply respecting Him. Our confession means being honest with Him—just as we are honest in relationships with others. Thanksgiving to Him means the attitude of appreciation. Seeking Him in supplication or petition shows that we trust Him to provide, knowing our needs are important to Him.

TOUGH TIMES

Do tough times and suffering affect our imaginations? Think of it this way: a tree is best measured when it is down. When we are felled by circumstances and events, we really find out what we are worth. Where do we turn for help in trouble? Do we selfishly want to control our own problems or do we surrender to God, in faith, knowing He will provide for us?

I know from personal experience that it is a gracious gift of God for us to suffer physically. I have struggled with broken legs. They take time to heal, and sometimes I have had to have further surgery. It is painful. It is frustrating. It tries my patience.

But these experiences have revealed more to me about the gracious provision of God. I have been able to grow closer to Him because I have learned to endure, and that has produced hope and love. It is frustrating when I am self-centered. It is a joyous experience when I look to Christ first.

But he said to me, "My grace is sufficient for you, for my power is made perfect in weakness." Therefore I will boast all the more gladly about my weaknesses, so that Christ's power may rest on me. That is why, for Christ's sake, I delight in weaknesses, in insults, in hardships, in persecutions, in difficulties. For when I am weak, then I am strong.

—2 Corinthians 12:9–10

Much of our growth comes from our trials. Suffering weans us from selfishness and makes us see God's grace more clearly. When life is difficult, we have the opportunity to grow deeper with God in the experience of obedience. We learn more about His love, His grace, His provision.

It does not always happen that way. Especially in difficult times, we are susceptible to negative thoughts and imaginations. We can feel abandoned by God and become angry and bitter, worried and depressed. But we are not alone. He has promised He will always be with us!

Who shall separate us from the love of Christ? Shall trouble or hardship or persecution or famine or naked-ness or danger or sword? As it is written: "For your sake we face death all day long; we are considered as sheep to be slaughtered." No, in all these things we are more than conquerors through him who loved us. For I am convinced that neither death nor life, neither angels nor demons, neither the present nor the future, nor any powers, neither height nor depth, nor anything else in all creation, will be able to separate us from the love of God that is in Christ Jesus our Lord.

—Romans 8:35–39

We will suffer in this life. We will experience pain and grief and loss. Members of our families may disappoint us with their behavior. We may struggle in a relationship with family or friends.

Our jobs won't always go well. But we will not suffer alone. We have the grace of God in our heart.

We must condition ourselves with this attitude in all tough times. C. K. Chesterton likened our trials to going through hot water:

- We must go through hot water. The good result is that we are cleaner.

- Genuine and fake diamonds look alike except under water. The genuine diamond still glows when submerged. The fake one is dull.

- The real joy in God is not diminished by troubles; it still sparkles.

We will be strengthened by tough times if we condition our mind to focus on God. If we are filled with His transforming faith, we will find rich blessings in adversity. But we must be vigilant in putting on the mind of Christ, rather than the worldly mind.

Howard Rutledge was one of many who served in Vietnam during the war and was captured by the North Vietnamese. Suffering while a prisoner, he found the Lord in a very real way. This time of great trouble gave him a great relationship with the Lord.

I have seen God at work in my own struggles as well. About thirty years ago, when I first started my medical practice in the Tampa Bay area, I developed a large referral practice with optometrists. Things have changed since then, but in those days, it was unheard of for ophthalmologists to take referrals from optometrists. Other ophthalmologists got upset that I was working with optometrists and they thought I was getting a bigger share of the "patient pie" than I should have. Their jealousy shaped me. It made me determined to do an excellent job, always performing far above anything that could be criticized.

I moved to a different area of Florida and established my practice there. I knew that if I did not move, the jealousies of my colleagues would hurt me. So I prayed for them and wished them well. I also used the situation to the glory of God and to the benefit of His kingdom. I dedicated my practice to God, and He has worked through me and the staff at St. Luke's to help thousands of patients through the years.

Imagine being in prison, charged falsely with a crime, not certain whether you will live or die. That was Paul's situation as he sat in a Roman jail, a prisoner of the Emperor Nero. Was he worried? Full of discouragement and doubt? Feeling weary and depressed? No. Here is how he described his attitude in a letter to his friends in Philippi:

> I will continue to rejoice, for I know that through your prayers and the help given by the Spirit of Jesus Christ, what has happened to me will turn out for my deliverance.
> —PHILIPPIANS 1:18–19

Paul did not say he would continue to endure his time in prison. Or that he would suffer but get through somehow, just suffering silently. Instead, he rejoiced! He delighted in the presence of God! And he commanded his friends:

> Rejoice in the Lord always. I will say it again: Rejoice!
> —PHILIPPIANS 4:4

Paul battled tough times with a "thanksgiving frenzy!" He worshiped His Savior! He taught us by example that whatever trouble any child of God faces, he or she is never alone. We can always rely on our Creator with a spirit of thanksgiving. Again, the apostle Paul encouraged this level of trust in time of trouble:

> We do not want you to be uninformed, brothers, about the hardships we suffered in the province of Asia. We were under great pressure, far beyond our ability to endure, so that we despaired even of life. Indeed, in our hearts we felt the sentence of death. But this happened

that we might not rely on ourselves but on God, who
raises the dead.

—2 CORINTHIANS 1:8–9

When things seem more than we can endure, God shows
us He will provide. We have His presence. And we can trust in
God, who is so powerful He can raise the dead. Like Paul, we can
find contentment in God, not in self and the world. This is Jesus'
promise to us:

I have told you these things, so that in me you may have
peace. In this world you will have trouble. But take heart!
I have overcome the world.

—JOHN 16:33

Know that whatever we face, Christ has faced it first. And He
has conquered it for us! The God of all grace gives us His grace
for each circumstance and trial—for financial trials, for family
trials, for relationship trials, for medical trials. For all areas of life,
God's grace is sufficient. May each of us see beyond sufferings
and trials to eternal glory. Paul explains it this way:

I consider that our present sufferings are not worth comparing with the glory that will be revealed in us.

—ROMANS 8:18

We may be tempted to focus on our current suffering, pain, and
disappointment. But we can counter those negative imaginations
with a focus on the glory that will be revealed in eternity. But not
just in eternity. We also have the Spirit's help, giving us hope and
faith in present times of suffering, which is really the glory of God
already in us. The glory has already begun. The glory is manifest in
us now! And we eagerly await its fullness in the future.

How do we get such glory? Through the Lord Jesus Christ.
Jesus acknowledged this reality to the Father when He prayed:

> I have given them the glory that you gave me, that they
> may be one as we are one: I in them and you in me.
> —JOHN 17:22–23

Now, we may not see this glory. Indeed, it is not externally visible to us in our current earthly condition. And it is certainly not visible to the world. Without looking through godly imaginations of Jesus, no one can see this glory. But through the process of maturing in our faith, it becomes more evident in our lives.

In the midst of trials, non-believers may ask why we seem at peace, why we have a positive attitude. They may wonder about the "pill" we are on. That "pill" is our faith in Christ. We know our needs have been supplied. We have nothing to prove to the world. We know who is in control, we know who is sovereign, we know who is our daily, and eternal, rest.

We need to think of our times of trouble and sorrow as times that prepare us, with great anticipation, for being engulfed in God's presence forever. That imagination will encourage us, motivate us, strengthen us, and support us. As we let our imaginations be focused on God in the present and in eternity, we put everything else in the background. Knowing God now as He is known in eternity provides us with peace during troubled times. Our faith in His promises and finding satisfaction in Him leads to overflowing peace.

FIGHTING DOUBT

Imagine you are being confronted by a hostile crowd, accusing you of being a follower of Christ. You are worried that they could arrest or even kill you. Would your faith sustain you in such a moment?

There are times when all of us doubt God's promises. If Peter, the foremost of the apostles, had doubts, why should we be any different? When we begin to experience doubt, we need to go back to the Word of God and re-read His promises. We need to spend time talking with God in prayer. We need to search out reinforcement with our Christian friends. We need to review our lives and remember the mighty things God has done for us. We need to remember the power of the loving one in whom we trust!

> Some trust in chariots and some in horses, but we trust in the name of the LORD our God.
>
> —PSALM 20:7

Faith is re-awakened when we realize His promises are true for each of us. Then our minds find their full satisfaction in Him. Our thoughts and actions are focused on Him. We glorify Him by being satisfied in Him.

> Though you have not seen him, you love him; and even though you do not see him now, you believe in him and are filled with an inexpressible and glorious joy, for you are receiving the goal of your faith, the salvation of your souls.
>
> —1 PETER 1:8–9

What a glorious promise! We believe without seeing, and that belief leads to our eternal life and salvation of our souls. It is common to wrestle with questions and doubts about God. "Who is our Creator? Does He live? Does He love? Does He forgive? Does He provide forever? How does He do it?"

The Old Testament tells us how Jacob wrestled:

> So Jacob was left alone, and a man wrestled with him till daybreak. When the man saw that he could not overpower him, he touched the socket of Jacob's hip so that his hip was wrenched as he wrestled with the man.
>
> —GENESIS 32:24–25

Still the man could not defeat Jacob. And Jacob would not let him go until he revealed himself. Finally the man blessed Jacob, and Jacob, who was renamed Israel, knew whom he had encountered:

I saw God face to face, and yet my life was spared.

—GENESIS 32:30

This is a picture of the kind of spiritual wrestling many of us encounter. Few of us become an "Israel" as a result of our wrestling. Few of us have an intimate physical encounter with God Almighty. But we still struggle. The result of wrestling for Jacob was a broken hip. He spent the rest of his life with a limp. Sometimes we are broken in some way as a result of our struggles. But when we are broken in the area of our pride, our selfishness, and our other sins, we can more fully submit our minds to God, and we become more effective as children of God.

We need to hold fast to our imagination of a life of faith, making faith the foundation upon which we build all our imaginations, refusing doubt. We cannot let the imaginations of this world detract from our focus on God. It is difficult to overcome the cares of this world—worries, coveting money, possessions, relationships, success. But remember, if our thoughts are not rooted in faith, they are sinful. They will destroy us. Instead, let us focus on the power and strength of the Almighty Lord. He overshadows any events and circumstances in this life on earth. He gives us new strength! Listen to the prophet, Isaiah:

> Do you not know? Have you not heard? The LORD is the everlasting God, the Creator of the ends of the earth. He will not grow tired or weary, and his understanding no one can fathom. He gives strength to the weary and increases the power of the weak. Even youths grow tired and weary, and young men stumble and fall; but those who hope in the LORD will renew their strength. They will soar on wings like eagles; they will run and not grow weary, they will walk and not be faint.
>
> —ISAIAH 40:28–31

We can feel overwhelmed by the struggles and battles in this world. But God understands. He created us. He knows us intimately. He walks with us every day. Turning to Him in faith will renew our strength and our energy. We are not alone! We have the power of the living God.

Getting Rid of Bad Thoughts

When we attempt to control our thoughts there are two approaches we can take—a negative one or a positive one. If we take the negative approach we might assert: "Oh, the heck with those thoughts," and then try to drive them out ourselves. Sometimes I have even pictured myself vomiting to rid myself of worldly thoughts. But this approach has a negative effect on one's whole personality and thought processes. When we erroneously think we can do it ourselves, we become critical. Negative ideas produce negative results.

The positive approach to controlling our thoughts is to turn the thoughts over to Jesus. We can say, "Jesus, take over this thought. Thank You for what You have given to me. I appreciate that You are taking care of this problem. Give me greater endurance and more godly character so I can have greater hope."

We need to cast out the parts of our life that produce worldly thoughts. We need to say goodbye to them and not return to them. Of course, we can only cast out these thoughts with the help of Christ. Once we are aware of wrong thoughts, we must quickly return our focus to God and cleanse our minds through His power.

> As a dog returns to its vomit, so a fool repeats his folly.
> —Proverbs 26:11

This verse condemns those as foolish who allow their minds to return to vain imaginations. Do we allow our minds to return to the "vomit"? Do we stay sick? Do we respond foolishly to our wrong thinking, opening up again the ungodly parts of our minds?

CHOOSING THE RIGHT COMPANIONS

I had an employee whom I hired shortly after her twentieth birthday. She was bright, beautiful, witty, and the daughter of a minister. She seemed to have everything going for her. Growing up in a Christian home, she accepted Christ as her personal Savior at an early age.

After moving to Florida with her family, she could not find the right peer group. While she still professed Christ as her Savior, she was no longer satisfied in Him. She became impatient for a romantic relationship in this new location where she did not have the support of her lifelong friends. It was not long before she became infatuated with a man considerably older than she. As a result, she found herself lying to her parents and seeing the man against their wishes. He was good looking and very persuasive. However, he challenged the very core of her beliefs and soon filled her mind with ungodly imaginations. He wooed her and convinced her of his supposedly undying love. It was not too long before he had her thinking his worldly thoughts about life.

Most of us know someone with a similar experience and the all-too-common ending to the familiar story. This bright, beautiful, witty daughter of a minister became pregnant. In mere months, her ungodly friend had influenced her imaginations and practically erased her values of a lifetime of Christian upbringing.

She was unable to resist temptation because her imaginations were no longer focused on Christ. If she had been satisfied in Christ, she would have been able to trust God with her desire for a romantic relationship. She would not have been deluded by false imaginations that caused her to be attracted to an ungodly man and then to commit sin.

Because of God's amazing grace, this story has a happy ending. The wonderful promise of 2 Chronicles 16:9 declares, "For the eyes of the LORD range throughout the earth to strengthen those whose hearts are fully committed to him." As this girl's family interceded in prayer and trusted God for His provision in their daughter's life, God's Spirit faithfully, gently brought back to her mind the imaginations of Christ and His redeeming love for her.

All the Scriptures and biblical principles she had learned throughout her childhood once again filled her mind. Her decision became clear: she would not marry this manipulative man; instead she would be a single mom and raise her child to know God. She confessed her sin, severed the relationship, and once again focused on Christ and His ability to provide for all her needs. Her imaginations were filled with dependence on the God who loved her so much that He forgave her.

Her immediate family, her church family, and her St. Luke's family stood with her and supported her decision. She gave birth to a wonderful, healthy baby boy, lived with her parents, and continued working at St. Luke's, all the while filling her mind with God's faithful promises that He would take care of her and her baby. And He did. Today, she is happily married, has another child, and is faithfully living for Jesus, totally committed to His purposes for her life. She chooses her friends very carefully and fills her family's life with people who love God.

It is important that we direct our thoughts toward God and keep them focused on Him. And it is equally important how we choose the people with whom we relate. People affect our thoughts. We should surround ourselves with people who are focused on God and want to grow in the Lord as much as we do. We have to be selective and sometimes say *no* to relationships with certain people—even if they seem exciting and interesting. True excitement and friendship come through sharing our lives in Jesus Christ. We cannot always choose whom we will spend our time with daily. But we can focus on sharing our lives—and our struggles—with those who are also seeking a closer relationship with God.

> My son, pay attention to what I say; listen closely to my words. Do not let them out of your sight, keep them within your heart; for they are life to those who find

them and health to a man's whole body. Above all else,
guard your heart, for it is the wellspring of life.

—PROVERBS 4:20–23

AVOIDING THE WRONG SITUATIONS

In addition to taking hold of our thoughts, we need to change
the actions that produce those thoughts. If there are places that
produce vain imaginations, we must avoid going to those places.
If there are activities and events that keep us from maturing in
Christ, we must choose not to participate. Anything that keeps us
from taking on the mind of Christ should be eliminated from our
lives. We must avoid putting ourselves in situations that compro-
mise our moral convictions. While we must be in the world, we
do not have to let the world be in us.

CHAPTER 19

A Cure for the Worry Disease

Are you worried right now? Are you afraid? Many of us face fears about economic problems or losses, physical distress, physical safety, or violence. Some people are worried or afraid all the time. *Anxiety* is the characteristic word for this age. And worry is one of the toughest battles we face in conditioning our minds.

As an ophthalmologist, I see patients every day. It is easy to identify the ones who are chronically worried. They are critical about the people and places around them. They are judgmental. They have trouble making decisions because worry preoccupies their minds. And worry affects their health. It makes them tired. It suppresses their immune systems, leaving them more susceptible to sickness and disease. Worry can destroy their entire bodies.

In the face of this dilemma, there is good news! God hears our cries. He will take care of us. If we have truly surrendered to Him and are resting in Him as Paul asserted he was doing in Galatians 2:20, there is no room for worry.

Consider what it would have been like to be Jabez, an Old Testament man. His mother named him Jabez, which sounds like the Hebrew word for pain, saying, "I gave birth to him in pain" (1 Chronicles 4:9). The Bible tells us that he was more honorable than his brothers. And he called on God:

> Jabez cried out to the God of Israel, "Oh, that you would bless me and enlarge my territory! Let your hand be with me, and keep me from harm so that I will be free from pain." And God granted his request.
>
> —1 CHRONICLES 4:10

God heard this man's supplication and granted it. He blessed Jabez, giving him pardon, peace, purpose, and power. God kept His hand on Jabez, protecting him and guiding him. From Genesis to Revelation, God promises to keep us in His hands. Those hands save us, heal us, carry us, care for us, support us, love us, redeem us, and sustain us. They are always with us. They will keep us for eternity. No matter how worn down and discouraged, how worried and anxious, we are still in His hands.

Is there anyone who has not experienced worry? Those who are rich worry that they are going to lose everything, and the poor worry that they aren't going to have enough. It is difficult to know who worries the most. But we do know who worries the least—the people who know their ultimate reality is both present and future grace in Jesus Christ. Jesus promises freedom from worry:

> "Come to me, all you who are weary and burdened, and I will give you rest. Take my yoke upon you and learn from me, for I am gentle and humble in heart, and you will find rest for your souls. For my yoke is easy and my burden is light."
> —MATTHEW 11:28–30

Faith is the reasonable response to revealed truth. When we believe God's promises are true for us, fear leaves. Worry leaves. Anxiety leaves. When our lives are centered on satisfaction in Him, we have peace that comes from knowing the sovereign God and understanding His almighty grace. Jesus gave us this wonderful promise:

> "Peace I leave with you; my peace I give you. I do not give to you as the world gives. Do not let your hearts be troubled and do not be afraid."
> —JOHN 14:27

True peace is based on our acceptance of the sovereignty of God. We aren't going to be able to explain God because we aren't

God. He is beyond our comprehension. We simply live by faith in our God who rules sovereignly in the affairs of men.

The peace of God silences the troubles in our spirits. Accepting the Gospel gives us a quiet heart. We get a clearer image of God as Jehovah-Shalom, the Lord is Peace. As we are filled with the Word of God, we are filled with the peace of God, which comes from worshiping God, trusting God, having God within us, and being in His kingdom of faith.

We need to integrate the concept of God's sovereignty into our lives. Then His grace is manifest, His future grace becomes our contemplation, and we find our right place with Him. He truly becomes our Father, our Provider, the Eternal One.

When we know God as Jehovah-Jireh, as our Father, and as our Shepherd, grace and peace are multiplied. Worry and other mind-sets of selfishness can no longer dominate our lives. He is the King and the Lord of our lives.

All things exist because of the power of God. We should stand in amazement and wonder at the power of the sovereign God. We have nothing to fear. Nevertheless, we tend to forget, at times, how powerful God is. He raised up Jesus! He has the power to do anything—even to destroy death, as Scripture clearly reveals:

> ...God who gives life to the dead and calls things that are not as though they were.
> —ROMANS 4:17

Actually, death could not hold God, in the person of Jesus, because He is by nature so powerful that it was impossible for death to hold Him. "The Spirit of him who raised Jesus from the dead is living in you" (Romans 8:11). That great power enables us to rise with Him. His power of resurrection becomes our power of eternal life.

There is a story about a couple who had been married many years when, tragically, the husband died in a drowning accident. His wife's comment was, "My God is in the heavens." She expressed her faith in God's sovereignty. She knew He would care for her. And she knew her husband was fellowshiping with God in heaven. Certainly she grieved over the loss of her husband. But she found comfort in the presence of the sovereign God.

Dr. Bob Morris says the more secure we are, the less we react to fear. When we are secure in Christ, we are not afraid. We must focus our minds on Christ, and He will help us feel secure, even in situations that could make us worry. God's plan is for us to be free from fear:

> For God did not give us a spirit of timidity, but a spirit of power, of love and of self-discipline.
>
> —2 TIMOTHY 1:7

We stand in victory over fear because of Calvary! We stand on the resurrection of our Lord Jesus Christ! Our confidence in Christ overcomes any insecurity, any worry, any fear. We are totally new beings in Him, and we know we will be with Him forever.

All of us should have such certainty in our faith. Yet there are times, even when we know God's presence is with us, that we struggle with fear and doubt. Even the disciples, who lived in the physical presence of Christ, were sometimes afraid:

> Then he got into the boat and his disciples followed him. Without warning, a furious storm came up on the lake, so that the waves swept over the boat. But Jesus was sleeping. The disciples went and woke him, saying, "Lord, save us! We're going to drown!" He replied, "You of little faith, why are you so afraid?" Then he got up and rebuked the winds and the waves, and it was completely calm. The men were amazed and asked, "What kind of man is this? Even the winds and the waves obey him!"
>
> —MATTHEW 8:23–27

The disciples were not securely confident of Jesus' sovereignty. They were frightened by the storm. Jesus had to remind them, once again, to have faith in Him. He demonstrated His mighty power over the storm, showing them that He was in control. And the disciples marveled at this man who calmed the water. If He can do that, how much more can He do?

In our lives, we will face storms of trouble. Now imagine Jesus with us in those storms, in our "boat" of life. He will calm the seas. He will calm our hearts. He has a commanding power over all the elements that affect our lives and toss us around every day. We should not focus on the storms. Instead, may we focus on His divine power that keeps us safe.

The disciples knew that the powerful storms on the sea of Galilee could take lives. In that same way, we all have been hurt by bad choices, bad experiences, bad relationships, even addictions. The results of those actions can destroy our confidence; they can damage our ability to trust in God. We can become insecure, angry, and fearful.

But remember, Christ loves us, even when we believe we are not worthy of that love. His grace is sufficient for all the thoughts and experiences in our lives. He will deliver us from desperate situations. He will meet all of our needs. He will restore us and renew our confidence when we place our trust in Him.

This is a lesson that the disciples struggled to learn. On another occasion, Jesus sent the disciples ahead of Him in a boat. After His time of prayer, He walked across the lake to them. The disciples were scared; they thought it was a ghost walking across the water. Jesus had to calm them down and tell them that it was Him. But Peter put Jesus to the test:

> "Lord, if it's you," Peter replied, "tell me to come to you on the water." "Come," he said. Then Peter got down out of the boat, walked on the water and came toward Jesus. But when he saw the wind, he was afraid and, beginning to sink, cried out, "Lord, save me!" Immediately Jesus reached out his hand and caught him. "You of little faith," he said, "why did you doubt?" And when they climbed into the boat, the

wind died down. Then those who were in the boat worshiped him, saying, "Truly you are the Son of God."

—MATTHEW 14:28–33

Peter could walk on the water as long as he trusted Jesus. But the wind shook his faith and he began to sink into the water. Once again, we see Jesus reaching out His mighty hand to save Peter. And Jesus will reach out to each of us, too. When the wind and the waves batter us, when we feel we are drowning and we begin to worry and feel afraid, we need to remember that He is there. His loving arms will keeps us safe. He is our confidence!

Trusting in those powerful arms is an important factor that prevents worry. We need to believe in God's sovereignty and in His power to care for us. The Bible tells us numerous times not to worry. We must trust in the Lord with all our hearts. He is the Almighty God. His power is limitless and His love for us is beyond measure! Jesus promised amazing power when we put our faith in Him:

> "Have faith in God," Jesus answered. "I tell you the truth, if anyone says to this mountain, 'Go, throw yourself into the sea,' and does not doubt in his heart but believes that what he says will happen, it will be done for him."
>
> —MARK 11:22–23

What a powerful promise God has made to His apostles! As we cultivate that kind of faith and trust, it will destroy any worry that creeps into our imaginations. Yet some people find it difficult to trust. They say, or at least think, "If you trust anyone, you are a fool." They tend to be skeptical, cynical, and adversarial in life's situations. These folks are living in a prison of their own making. Richard Lovelace wrote, in his poem *To Althea from Prison* in 1649, "Stone walls do not a prison make."

Fear. Doubt. Worry. These are the building blocks that will imprison us. We can become slaves to our emotions. They affect our relationships with others. Most importantly, they affect our relationship with God.

149

If we have trouble trusting people, whom we see and with whom we come into physical contact, we have even greater trouble trusting God, whom we cannot see. Those truly imprisoned by fear and worry see no evidence of God in their lives. They might go through the motions of asking Him for help, but they doubt that He will actually provide all they need.

> He who doubts is like a wave of the sea, blown and tossed by the wind. That man should not think he will receive anything from the Lord; he is a double-minded man, unstable in all he does.
>
> —JAMES 1:6–8

Doubt destroys the satisfaction we find in God's promises. It causes us to lose our image of God as Creator and Provider and we no longer have a mind-set of trust. Our foundation of faith is shaky. We will not conquer worry until we focus on the person of Jesus Christ. Remember, the Lord-Jireh will provide for all those who put their faith in Him. When we find satisfaction in His provision, when we turn our minds to imagining His promises, when we worship Him as the disciples did, we will be freed from worry. And we are filled with His peace.

When I begin to worry, I picture myself being in God's heaven, running through the clouds with some of the people who were great runners. Of course, I will be far behind them. Their style and technique are far greater than mine. But I imagine running through those golden streets of heaven in a state of maximum love with my Lord.

Those imaginations allow me to focus on His future grace, a grace that will allow me to be with Him and experience His care for eternity. Our eternal life in that kingdom is the greatest assurance of peace for the present. We worry less about the circumstances and events of this world because we know a greater world. We are transformed because we have confidence in Christ. This imagination demolishes worry!

CHAPTER 20

Numbered With the Transgressors

We can look to Jesus as our role model of a satisfied mind. But some may wonder, because He was divine, if it was easier for Him to be abandoned to God. The prophet Isaiah reminds us that Jesus also was human and that He had very human struggles:

> He had no beauty or majesty to attract us to him, nothing in his appearance that we should desire him. He was despised and rejected by men, a man of sorrows, and familiar with suffering. Like one from whom men hide their faces he was despised, and we esteemed him not.
>
> —ISAIAH 53:2–3

Jesus never "took the easy way out" during His life on earth. According to the Scriptures, he was not particularly handsome, which would have helped Him get some attention. More than that, He did not have a very pleasant life. He did not have a home, a regular place to sleep, and He had to live from the generosity of others. Many people had a very low opinion of Him—they were not very generous. Yet, Jesus displayed His mercy to all:

> While Jesus was having dinner at Matthew's house, many tax collectors and "sinners" came and ate with him and his disciples. When the Pharisees saw this, they asked his disciples, "Why does your teacher eat with tax collectors and 'sinners'?" On hearing this, Jesus said, "It is not the healthy who need a doctor, but the sick. But go and learn

151

what this means: 'I desire mercy, not sacrifice.' For I have not come to call the righteous, but sinners."

—MATTHEW 9:10–13

Jesus is our Doctor. He understands our sinful condition. He knows how to heal our wounds and give peace to our souls. But He does not act solely from a clinical, objective viewpoint. He is intimately acquainted with mankind's suffering. Isaiah describes Jesus' own suffering and how that intimately binds us to Him:

> Therefore I will give him a portion among the great, and he will divide the spoils with the strong, because he poured out his life unto death, and was numbered with the transgressors. For he bore the sin of many, and made intercession for the transgressors.
>
> —ISAIAH 53:12

Christ was numbered with us; He was considered one of us. Christ was bruised and beaten for us. He was crucified for us. Through His suffering, He was bound together with our suffering. My heart overflows with love and gratitude from that image of a suffering Christ. He took my sins and paid for them with His own blood. He healed me and restored me to relationship with God the Father. He redeemed me with His precious blood. There is no greater satisfaction possible than having that relationship restored. He loved me so much that He paid a great price for me. And I live in His provision now and for eternity because He bound Himself to suffering humanity.

When each of us finds our full measure of satisfaction in the grace of our glorious Lord, we must follow Christ's pattern and bind ourselves with our fellow sinners. We need to allow compassion for hurting humanity to fill our hearts. In living out our image of Christ, we need to be bound with all other people who sin—and that is everyone. Even our fellow believers in Christ sin at times. Non-believers sin. All of us are sinners. There are no exceptions. It is only through Christ's grace that we are saved. We cannot earn our own salvation, nor can we expect others to earn their salvation.

So we must consider ourselves, as having the mind of Christ, to be "numbered with the transgressors" as He was. We need to be filled with compassion, given to intercession, never becoming the accusers of another. It is our responsibility to suffer with others and feel their burdens as Christ suffered for us.

A young man I know is one of the best examples of leading a life that is "numbered with the transgressors." He manages an office building for me. His wife's family has been involved in the Christian musical world for many years. They have three wonderful boys.

This young man extends himself to people who have been in all kinds of trouble—drug and alcohol abusers, thieves and con-artists. He does more than wish them well; he brings them into his home, ministers to them, suffers with them. Sometimes, he even suffers because of them. Yes, these folks occasionally have stolen from him. Once, someone took something he valued greatly and sold it to get money to buy drugs. Yet, I have seen this man accept these "transgressors" back into his house and family even after they have sinned against him. He keeps on loving them and persevering because he never thinks of himself as better than they are. He considers himself an equal transgressor.

I have tried to help some doctors who were kicked out of the medical society. I thought they were good doctors who just had difficulty in understanding people. And sometimes, I was hurt by them after expending efforts to help them.

It does not always work out well when we try to help others. We may try to help people, only to have them take our money and never return it. Or, we may try to help those who have substance abuse problems, only to have them leave us hurt, confused, and disappointed. Often the cost for being numbered with the transgressors is high.

Six or seven years ago, a doctor who worked with me abandoned his wife and kids. He married a second time, then divorced that wife and married for a third time. He and his third wife had a child. While all this was happening, I responded somewhat arrogantly toward him. I emotionally distanced myself from the situation and tried not to care about whether or not he was destroying himself. Then I realized that I, too, could have been in a similar situation except for the grace of God. In a deeper way, I realized how we are to number ourselves with transgressors.

To allow ourselves to be numbered with the transgressors involves more than intellectually trying to help someone. It involves the deep realization that we could be, and possibly are, vulnerable to the same sins as others whose lives we observe. We can, and do, fail. We are all sinners in God's eyes.

Recently, another friend of mine abandoned his family. Then he got involved in another relationship that was obviously going to end badly. Instead of my former arrogant response, I decided to "number myself" with him. I contacted one of his closest friends, and the three of us started spending time together. We let him know we were with him and felt his suffering, confusion, and pain. And we prayed for him. This man was restored to his wife, and he has a much stronger marriage now. The life lesson for me is to choose to relate to others humbly and reach out to them in love.

Paul, the great apostle, missionary, preacher, and writer probably had more reason than most to feel slightly arrogant from his position of authority in the church. But he did not. In one incident he revealed his humility by identifying with a runaway slave, Onesimus, who had robbed his master and escaped to Rome. In Rome, through Paul's ministry, he became a follower of Christ.

Paul knew Onesimus had run away and that it was the necessary time for him to return to his master and pay the debt he owed him. His owner, Philemon, was a fairly prominent man in the city of Colossae. He was also a follower of Christ, and Paul considered him a good friend. So Paul sent Onesimus back, with a letter in hand, which became one of Paul's epistles included in the Scriptures. He charged Philemon, regarding Onesimus:

> If he has done you any wrong or owes you anything, charge it to me...I will pay it back.
>
> —PHILEMON 1:18–19

Paul asked Philemon to spare Onesimus and was willing to becoming responsible personally for his debts. He entreats Philemon as a friend:

> So if you consider me a partner, welcome him [Onesimus] as you would welcome me.
>
> —PHILEMON 1:17

It is clear from this passage that Paul considered himself equal with Onesimus, a runaway slave. But that is not to say he considered Onesimus as good as he. Rather, he understood he was an equal sinner to Onesimus. He lived out the attitude of Christ that he described in his letter to the church at Philippi:

> Who, being in very nature God, did not consider equality with God something to be grasped, but made himself nothing, taking the very nature of a servant, being made in human likeness.
>
> —PHILIPPIANS 2:6–7

Paul tells us that we should have the same attitude as Christ revealed. We are to serve others, knowing that we are not better than they are, but that we are all equal. Christ makes us equal. All who are saved are saved by His matchless, boundless grace alone!

Chapter 21

Letting Our Light Shine

If we are truly satisfied with God's promises, can we still demonstrate a negative attitude? How is our attitude affected by our level of satisfaction? How does our daily life unfold if we are feeling positive? How about when we are feeling negative?

The Bible tells us what our attitude should be when we focus on walking with God every day:

> Blessed are those who have learned to acclaim you, who walk in the light of your presence, O Lord. They rejoice in your name all day long; they exult in your righteousness.
> —Psalm 89:15–16

These verses tell us that our attitude will be one of joy and rejoicing when we are truly satisfied with God's promises. When we walk in the light of God's presence we are no longer negative and critical people. We might describe this difference in attitude as the difference between becoming a "light" or remaining a "shadow." As we consider the wonderful concept of *light* as revealed in the Scriptures, we will see whether or not we qualify as those who are letting our light shine.

In the Scriptures, the term *light* is used in different ways. First and foremost, Christ uses this word to describe Himself:

> I am the light of the world. Whoever follows me will never walk in darkness, but will have the light of life.
> —John 8:12

Light carries the meaning of illuminating and brightening everything around us; it refers to being informed or enlightened as well. In contrast to the life and understanding that light brings, *shadows* could be described as taking them away. Shadows make objects difficult to see and concepts difficult to understand. Jesus not only referred to Himself as light, he also instructs His followers to live lives characterized by light:

> You are the light of the world.
> —MATTHEW 5:14

Our light is the light of Christ shining through us. We are like the moon, reflecting the light of the sun. On our own, we give little light. But when we align with the Son, we can radiate a powerful light in the earth. We shine with God's truth, reflecting His love. Paul explains how we can be lights in this dark, confusing world:

> Do everything without complaining or arguing, so that you may become blameless and pure, children of God without fault in a crooked and depraved generation, in which you shine like stars in the universe.
> —PHILIPPIANS 2:14–15

Let me give you an example. At a recent conference I attended, many of the physicians were complaining about how insurance reimbursements for cataract surgery had been cut 60 percent in the past ten years. I certainly sympathized with their complaints. Many of us have done more work for which we made less money during the last ten years. As I listened to the doctors' complaints that day, it seemed that they were feeding each others' unhappiness. And I realized just how important it is to have a good attitude toward difficult situations in life.

As I looked around at the doctors who were complaining, they did not look as though they had physically suffered because of their drop in income. When it was my turn to contribute,

I suggested that we should be thankful that through medical advances we can now help people in a greater way.

We need to consider how to be lights who offer praise, encouragement, and appreciation rather than shadows who are negative, critical, and selfish. Do we love our work and display a positive attitude, or do we resent our work, displaying ingratitude, lack of motivation, and a generally poor attitude?

What about our relationships with others? Do we contribute positively or negatively in relationships? Do we appreciate our children and their status in life? Do we encourage them or criticize them? Do we enjoy their presence? Do we treat our spouses as partners or as marital servants to be ordered about, rather than loved and appreciated?

Clebe McClary excellently exemplifies a Christ-centered attitude. He is an accomplished marathon runner who can stay on a treadmill longer than just about anyone in his age group. His feats are even more remarkable because he lives his life without one arm and one eye. In his book, *Living Proof*, he reveals the secret to his positive attitude: "In this world of give and take, there are not enough people who are willing to give what it takes," he says.[1]

A God-centered attitude must be joined to a proper estimation of our abilities. (See Romans 12:3.) For example, we may have a positive attitude that we are going to get in a boxing ring and face Muhammad Ali in his prime, but we're going to take a licking. Our abilities must be developed to go along with our attitude. Our faith is rooted in the blessings we receive as the children of God, and one of those blessings is His enablement. (See Philippians 4:13.) We focus on the positive imaginations of Christ. It's more than thinking random good thoughts and hoping vaguely for the best. We are taking on the mind of Christ.

The foundation for a positive attitude is our unshakable faith in God's provision.

And we know that in all things God works for the good
of those who love him, who have been called according
to his purpose.

—ROMANS 8:28

One of the great ophthalmologists in our era is Dr. Jim Rowsey, whom I consider to be a great "light" in his ministry. He is a
man who truly loves God and lives according to His purpose. Dr.
Rowsey is the physician who treated the very first patient in the
United States with the VISX-Tauton Excimer Laser to provide
FDA approval. He is the VISX principal certifying surgeon in the
state of Florida, and has trained more eye surgeons to perform
refractive surgery than any other clinician in the state. Dr. Rowsey designed the first computerized corneal topography device
for measuring refractive surgery results.

He loves his work as an ophthalmologist. His enthusiasm and
excitement are contagious. In meetings, he consistently offers a
positive way to solve problems. A difficult diagnosis is always a
challenge, not a defeat. If one treatment does not work, he considers alternate management of the medical problem. In surgery, he
always looks for a better way to care for patients.

Dr. Rowsey's enthusiasm and joyous attitude are displayed in
all areas of his life. He says joy comes to us as we share it. He
firmly believes that a spirit of joy in our life shines out and affects
everyone around us. He says, "When I have ten phone calls to
return at the end of the day, I have made a decision to smile at the
telephone before I dial the phone (though it has never smiled back
at me) and to continue smiling as the phone is ringing. When the
call is answered, my expressed joy at hearing the patient's voice is
recognized by the patient as they answer the phone."

He tells a beautiful illustration of exactly how this decision to
be filled with joy works in his life and affects others. He accompa-
nied his three-year-old granddaughter to the ice-skating rink for
one of her first lessons. As they together crept around the edge of
the ice rink, holding onto the railing, she fell down every foot or

so. Each time, she valiantly pulled herself back up, grabbing the rail with both hands.

She was undaunted by the trauma of continuous "defeat" and began singing throughout the ordeal, "I have the JOY, JOY, JOY, JOY down in my heart…" She sang over and over again with each fall. As she labored around the rink with her grandfather, she spotted an elderly man standing by the side of the rink, scowling at the display of skaters. It was obvious that he was not enjoying himself. Skating right in front of him, she took another fall. For the umpteenth time, she pulled herself up, looked up, and sang right into the scowling man's face. "I have the JOY, JOY, JOY, JOY down in my heart…"

Suddenly the scowling man's frown was transformed into a big smile! He couldn't help it, as he recognized the little girl's decision to keep singing in the face of falling. He caught the contagious joy from a little one determined to sing and smile regardless of her dismal circumstance.

Each of us can become light and joy to others, showing a Christlike attitude from imaginations that are filled with His Word:

> Be joyful always; pray continually; give thanks in all circumstances, for this is God's will for you in Christ Jesus.
> —1 THESSALONIANS 5:16–18

Our challenge every day is to align our imaginations with Christ. As we have discussed, our pure and complete satisfaction comes from believing His promises and following His commandments—acting out His commandments in our lives. It is not enough for our minds to contain the thoughts; we must live in the attitude of expressing and fulfilling God's promises:

> Do not conform any longer to the pattern of this world, but be transformed by the renewing of your mind. Then you will be able to test and approve what God's will is— his good, pleasing and perfect will.
> —ROMANS 12:2

God is most glorified when we are satisfied in Him. Every day, let us seek His mind, His heart, His joy, and His peace. Every day, let us seek His pure and perfect will. Every day, let us rejoice in the eternal promises He has made us. Every day, let us find our *shalom* in our relationship with Him.

CHAPTER 22

Abandoned to God

I am not much of a golfer, but I have played a few rounds through the years. If I have learned anything from playing golf it is that if I imagine that I can play well and am satisfied with my performance, I usually have a good game. But if I become frustrated with the game and have images of not putting well, I usually fulfill that image. Of course, my skill level determines to some extent my performance. But I have learned that more important than my skill level is the attitude I bring to the game.

My imaginations affect how well I perform. I can choose to try and play the perfect game and never be happy while I am on the course. I can be negative, criticizing and second-guessing every move. Or I can find satisfaction in just being out there, doing my best, and enjoying my efforts.

This lesson of the importance of attitude does not apply solely to golf. A sense of satisfaction in my daily life, rooted in godly imaginations, is essential if I am going to find a peaceful and joyous life filled with meaningful relationships and actions.

As we mature in our faith and develop an eternal mind-set, our daily lives should reflect our change of attitude. Faith in the promises of God should radiate through us as we put Jesus at the center of our lives. He is reflected in all our thoughts and actions. Think of it like this: we should be so absorbed with the Savior that if we were cut anywhere, Jesus Christ would be seen.

We find a mature sense of satisfaction that comes from spiritual wisdom. True spiritual wisdom involves faith in the promises of God and sees their truth for each of us. We act on those promises, and our actions produce fruitful lives.

This satisfaction is more that just a general feeling of content-ment or well-being. It comes from believing the promises of God and finding fulfillment and purpose in those promises. I need to be continually satisfied with the life God has given me in Christ Jesus, with His provision for my daily physical, spiritual, intellec-tual, and emotional needs. In that way I develop a God-centered mind-set, based on my satisfaction in Him. The Scripture prom-ises this wonderful satisfaction:

> Let them give thanks to the LORD for his unfailing love and his wonderful deeds for men, for he satisfies the thirsty and fills the hungry with good things.
> —PSALM 107:8–9

If I develop a sense of satisfaction about my golf game and let my performance ride on that satisfaction, I perform at a higher level. I certainly get the most out of my abilities, no matter how limited they are. And my apparent satisfaction in the game spreads to those around me, making for an enjoyable outing.

Consider for a moment your "golf game." Is satisfaction in God's promises the foundation for all your relationships? When we are totally satisfied in Christ, we are abandoned to Him. As we learned in our discussion of John Wesley's transformation, what we truly know is what we live.

As we live our lives, recognizing our bodies are temples of the Holy Spirit, He flows His light and life through us, transform-ing us, taking us from glory to greater glory. Our actions should reflect those of a faithful steward who wants to carry out the work of the Master, our Lord.

The famous coach for the Green Bay Packers, Vince Lombardi, encouraged his players to "run with abandonment." As Chris-tians, the only way we can run with abandonment is to be at total peace with the Lord. We surrender all our fears and anxieties and choose to depend on His sovereignty for our future, His love for our present, His mercy for our past. And we focus on our eternal future with Him.

That's not to say we have to have a cheerleader mentality, in which we say, "Oh yes, yes!" Running with abandonment is simply being totally focused on the Lord, with our imaginations forming the foundation of a God-centered attitude. Of course, I am not advocating an attitude that declares we are not sick if we really are. But a God-centered attitude, in the midst of difficulties, will declare: "I'm sick, but my sickness is in the Lord's hands and He is my Healer!" We simply call on the Lord in trouble, as the psalmist did:

> The LORD is near to all who call on him, to all who call on him in truth. He fulfills the desires of those who fear him; he hears their cry and saves them.
>
> —PSALM 145:18–19

What a beautiful image: God is near us. He is a God who is close to us on a personal basis. We are engulfed with Him, we are intimate with Him, we feel His presence. We can sincerely and ardently call on Him because we believe He will provide help for us. This honest cry forms the foundation for our God-centered attitude.

When we are abandoned to God, we have total trust and faith in God, which allows us to live without worry, to live with a mind-set of godly joy. And we have total release from ourselves to love God. Our faith permeates every aspect of our lives.

> I have set the LORD always before me. Because he is at my right hand, I will not be shaken.
>
> —PSALM 16:8

Some may consider this a radical attitude, putting God emphatically at the center of one's life. But I have found there is no other way to know satisfaction. With God at the center, joy and peace flow out of me like spokes going out from the hub of a wheel. I am loving, I am thankful. Like you, I still struggle with overcoming doubt at times. At those times, I go back to God's Word for encouragement, for guidance, for support, for reassurance, for hope.

Picture throwing a rock into a quiet pond. Waves of water ripple from that one simple act. In that same way, seeking complete satisfaction in the promises of God has a ripple effect throughout our life. Understanding some of the wonderful, divine attributes of God will teach us how they can affect our lives.

A SUPERNATURAL GOD

First of all, God is a Creator. Imagining God and His ability to create and sustain all the intricacies of the world should cause us to stand in amazement and wonder. How great this God is!

Let's consider one of the more simple structures in the universe—a single cell. The great physiologists may study its minute structure, even down to its different proteins, but they still cannot answer all the questions about how this single cell functions. They do not know why its proteins behave the way they do, what energizes them, what makes them become signal proteins. The attempt to answer these questions leads us deeper into the mystery of its creation. Eventually we come to the realization that no one can answer the ultimate questions of life: Who is God; what is creation; what is man; what is the single cell?

As a young medical student, I studied single-cell metabolism and felt I qualified as a molecular biologist. I even tried to write a book on the subject, but soon realized I did not know a whole lot about what made the single cell function. The more I studied, the more I understood that even the most brilliant scientists do not fully understand the amazing function of a simple, single cell. That realization was instrumental in leading me to God. The awesome creation of a single cell was reason enough to believe in Him.

God is greater than any of the physical laws of the universe that we know. His power transcends all of our understanding of those laws. By definition, the supernatural transcends the natural, has power over it, and is not limited to it.

There are people who try to fit God within the natural laws He created and admit no divine intervention. Some great scientists do not acknowledge any supernatural powers and think only of the power of natural laws, not the supernatural. But author William Lane Craig looks at the concept of the supernatural as a theologian. He says we must look at our God as supernatural, with powers greater than the natural laws, having control over natural laws, but not limited to them or by them.[1]

It is this supernatural attribute of God that gives us freedom from worry and fear. Because of His supernatural power, we know He can do all things.

A MERCIFUL JUDGE

God's mercy is founded upon justice. God is a Judge who sits upon the highest throne. His justice is executed upon sin at the cross where Jesus Christ died. His almighty wrath was poured out on the Lord Jesus so that we could receive mercy. The apostle Paul declares:

> This righteousness from God comes through faith in Jesus Christ to all who believe...and are justified freely by his grace through the redemption that came by Christ Jesus. God presented him as a sacrifice of atonement, through faith in his blood. He did this to demonstrate his justice.
>
> —ROMANS 3:22–25

A holy God demands judgment for sin. Christ's death on the cross completely satisfied the righteousness of a holy God, making it possible for Him to show mercy righteously to sinful mankind. Those who believe, therefore, are treated as righteous because Christ bore their sins.

Through His death on the cross, Christ gives righteousness as a gift to all who come to Him in faith. It is only through Christ's righteousness that we can be declared righteous. The mercy we receive at the cross is founded upon God's justice.

A Loving Heart

Jonathan Edwards talks about love as being one of the "essentials" of God. Indeed, this assertion is based on Scripture, which declares: God is love. (See 1 John 4:8.) And Romans 8:31–32 tells us that His love overflows His sovereignty:

> What then shall we say to these things? If God is for us, who can be against us? He who did not spare His own Son, but delivered Him up for us all, how shall He not, with Him also freely give us all things?
> —Romans 8:31–32, NKJV

The Gospel of John declares:

> For God so loved the world that he gave his one and only Son, that whoever believes in him shall not perish but have eternal life.
> —John 3:16

The love of God is not an intellectual love; it is love that greatly desires relationship with us. The life of King David holds many examples for us of God's love. Though David had many spiritual ups and downs, it is apparent that one thing he knew was the "Father heart" of God. He intimately experienced God's love and forgiveness. Many times he stood in awe and admiration of God's mercy to him.

In the story of David's sin with Bathsheba and his murder plot against Uriah (see 2 Samuel:12), the prophet Nathan finally helped David see the magnitude of his sins. And David confessed: "I have sinned against the LORD" (2 Samuel 12:13). Could David ever believe he could be forgiven of his enormous sins?

Perhaps not. But the loving heart of God responded immediately to David's confession, through the prophet, Nathan:

> The LORD has taken away your sin. You are not going
> to die.
>
> —2 SAMUEL 12:13

David knew God's mercy was greater than his own sin. He knew God as his heavenly Father; he knew his Father's heart and his Father's love. Later, David experienced fatherly love of his own when his son Absalom rebelled against him and drove David out of Jerusalem. In the power struggle that followed, Absalom was killed (2 Samuel 18:9–15). Though Absalom had sinned cruelly against David, the fatherly love David had for his rebellious son caused him to weep and mourn deeply upon his death:

> The king was shaken. He went up to the room over the
> gateway and wept. As he went, he said: "O my son Absa-
> lom! My son, my son Absalom! If only I had died instead
> of you—O Absalom, my son, my son!"
>
> —2 SAMUEL 18:33

God's loving heart reveals an even greater depth of love and forgiveness—the supernatural, Father heart of God.

OUR LIBERTY

When God is our portion, the veil over our hearts is taken away. We have the liberty of the Lord to behold Him with an unshrouded face. Our blindness is lifted, and we are able to come face to face spiritually before God, according to the Scriptures:

> Now the Lord is the Spirit, and where the Spirit of the
> Lord is, there is freedom. And we, who with unveiled
> faces all reflect the Lord's glory, are being transformed

into his likeness with ever-increasing glory, which comes
from the Lord, who is the Spirit.

—2 Corinthians 3:17–18

Our liberty in Christ does not mean license to live selfishly;
it involves living by the commands of Christ. Jesus Himself
describes this liberty, using the farming imagery of being yoked
together with Him, like two oxen pulling a plow. Then He says,
"My yoke is easy and my burden is light" (Matthew 11:30).

The liberty of knowing our bounds in Christ frees us. We do
what we want to do because our bounds are already set in Christ.
In Christ, we learn to see the transcience of the old and we know
the glory and freedom of the new.

The New Testament puts a special emphasis on the soul being
liberated from the bondage of sin. When we realize we have a
position of freedom in God, nothing can intimidate us. Nothing
can ensnare us. Nothing has a grip on our lives but Christ. Christ
has liberated us from sin; we can serve Him with fountains of joy,
as the Scriptures affirm:

> It is for freedom that Christ has set us free. Stand firm,
> then, and do not let yourselves be burdened again by a
> yoke of slavery.
>
> —Galatians 5:1

The importance of the ceremonial laws and rituals in the Old
Testament is that they are pointers to Christ. However, from man-
made rules, which lead to bondage, we are set free. The heart of
faith and the life of liberty lived unto God become our priority,
according to the Scriptures:

> For in Christ Jesus neither circumcision nor uncircum-
> cision has any value. The only thing that counts is faith
> expressing itself through love.
>
> —Galatians 5:6

GOD AT WORK THROUGH US

As we have discussed, our godly focus affects all the areas of our lives—our emotions, our actions, our relationships, our career, our attitudes. As God loves us, we learn to love others. As God is gracious to us, we are gracious to others. As He is merciful to us, we are merciful to others. As He forgives us, we forgive others. These attributes of God become our own; they merge and overlap in us and we reflect God's love to the people in our lives. When we let His thoughts be our thoughts, we are filled with a total *shalom*, a divine peace that leads to imaginations focused on our eternal relationship with Christ.

When I let my mind be filled with imaginations of God, glorifying and worshiping Him, I find joy in my life every day. True joy depends on total abandonment to God and His sovereignty. Christ describes our relationship as joy being made full. We have a new spirit of joy, of love, of forgiveness, of peace, and of generosity. We have new imaginations that transform us internally and change the quality of our relationships with others.

Satan would love to undermine who we are as believers. He would love for us to feel defeated in bad times. He would love for us to be shaky in our faith and forget to focus on God, in good times as well as bad. But Jesus provides our stability. When we feel weak in our faith, we call on Him and seek His presence. He will help us regain our strength and stand firm. Listen to the encouragement of Moses to Joshua:

> Then Moses summoned Joshua and said to him in the presence of all Israel, "Be strong and courageous, for you must go with this people into the land that the LORD swore to their forefathers to give them...The LORD himself goes before you and will be with you; he will never leave you nor forsake you. Do not be afraid; do not be discouraged."
>
> —DEUTERONOMY 31:7–8

Our strength does not come from worldly thinking. We have a new vision of God leading us. He is our banner before us, guiding us. Just as He fulfilled His promise to lead the Israelites and give them a new home, He will lead each of us. He is with us, He abides in us, we are engulfed or wrapped up in Him.

Have you faced bitterness, resentment, pride, anger, or worry? Each of us must choose to focus on Christ and bring the mind into union with His divine knowledge. Seeking the mind of Christ will keep us from self-destruction through our own greed, insecurity, jealousy, and other harmful thinking. When Christ is fixed in our thoughts, worldly imaginations cannot easily creep in. We are filled with the Holy Spirit and attitudes that develop from a mind focused on God. Consider whether your life reflects that fruit:

> But the fruit of the Spirit is love, joy, peace, patience, kindness, goodness, faithfulness, gentleness and self-control.
>
> —GALATIANS 5:22–23

The fruit of the Spirit is God at work in us, producing the supernatural attributes of Christ in our lives. We cannot develop these qualities fully by ourselves, but only through our union with Christ. Our joy is a joy in Him. Our peace is His *shalom* in our hearts. When we focus on Him in everything we do, we can be filled with positive imaginations. We love others; we are humble; we are cooperative; we are flexible; we work with others rather than against them. And we choose constructive solutions rather than destructive criticism.

Perhaps you can think of your attitude as a building block. We can take a block and throw it through a window or we can use it to rebuild broken walls. A negative attitude will destroy us and those around us, while a positive attitude based on the imaginations of Christ will strengthen us and help us love and appreciate others.

Mr. Blancher is a man who was serving in the armed forces and was stationed in Florida. While there, he went to the library to read books. One book he was reading had many notes written in the margins. They seemed to be written by someone with great insight and beauty. He read the book in a week, and then re-read it because of the additional comments in the notes that enriched his understanding.

Mr. Blancher decided to try to find the writer of the notes. Learning the book had been donated to the library by a woman in New York, he wrote to her and told her how much her notes had meant to him. He did not expect any response. But surprisingly, he received a letter from the note-writer. They struck up a wonderful correspondence, which continued while Mr. Blancher served overseas. He shared his fears about serving in the war and she comforted him, telling him that all great men are scared at one time or another.

She reminded him that the words of Psalm 23 told him he could prevail without fear, even through the valley of the shadow of death, because the Lord would be with him and His mighty hand would uphold him. Mr. Blancher looked forward to her letters because of her strong, thoughtful comments. But he never asked for a picture of her because he did not want appearances to affect their relationship. If she were attractive, he was afraid he would continue writing for other reasons than her helpful comments. If she were unattractive, he was afraid he might pity her and quit sharing his thoughts, or that he would lose interest in her.

After returning from his military service, Mr. Blancher traveled to New York. He arranged to meet his "pen pal" for the first time at Grand Central Station, followed by dinner together. She was to wear a red rose so that he could recognize her in the crowd. When he arrived at the station, he saw a beautiful woman walking toward him. She was more electrifying and alive than he had ever hoped his writer would be. She smiled when she saw him, then walked by. There was no red rose.

Across the way he saw the woman with the rose. Immediately, he concluded she was about fifty years old, and noted she was wearing very conservative clothes; her hair was graying. She didn't appear to belong in New York. Still, he went over to her and introduced himself. He told her how happy he was to finally meet her and how much he had enjoyed her letters through the years. He said he would be honored to take her to dinner.

The woman appeared a bit confused. She replied that a young lady had given her the rose and asked her to wear it. The young lady had also told her that if a soldier came by and asked her to dinner, she should send him to the restaurant across the street. The young woman would be waiting there. Startled, Mr. Blancher thanked the lady with the rose, and turned to walk across the street to the restaurant to which she had pointed.

Sure enough, waiting in the restaurant was the young woman he had seen in the train station earlier.

Mr. Blancher's focus on heart issues made the difference in his relationship with his pen pal. He was committed to knowing his letter writer's heart, not judging her by her appearance. Otherwise, he would have been acutely disappointed that the woman with the rose wasn't the beautiful young woman he had noticed earlier.

Instead, he treasured a relationship with the inner beauty of the person that had been revealed through years of correspondence. He knew that God doesn't judge us by our appearances but by the heart, and he sought to do the same. As a result he ended up meeting a beautiful woman after all.

What about us? How often do our attitudes reflect the love of Christ? How often are we open to being positive people who focus on Jesus first, letting His love strengthen our relationships with others? Are we inclined to bolster others or to battle them? To reassure or resent? To nurture or nag?

To run with abandon, we must be aligned with God. Hebrews 12:2 says, "Let us fix our eyes on Jesus." Attitude begins with our mind-set. When we focus first on Christ, a Christlike attitude will fill us. We are filled with His light. Gone is a spirit of criticism and condemnation. Instead, we become constructive people who believe life is full of God's blessings.

Our perception changes when we no longer look at the bad circumstances and events in our life, giving in to discouragement with them. No longer do we wallow in pity, anger, or bitterness.

When we trust in God we have a new attitude, a new perception and a new hope, as the Bible promises:

> May the God of hope fill you with all joy and peace as you trust in him, so that you may overflow with hope by the power of the Holy Spirit.
>
> —ROMANS 15:13

Hope is to the human mind and soul what air is to the lungs. Without hope we cannot "breathe" spiritually. Hope is absolutely essential to the human spirit. Our quality of life is dependent upon hope.

We may search for hope in all kinds of ways. It is essential, therefore, that we see the difference between the false hope that the world offers and the genuine hope of God. Genuine hope is based on the promises of God. These promises allow a subjective confidence to grow within us, especially as we read them over and over in His Word. They are to be applied to each part of the spirit, mind, and body.

When facing difficult circumstances we may begin to doubt God's promises. At those times, we need to go back, read His promises in His Word, examine our lives to see how He has provided for us in the past, and actually preach to ourselves that the promises of God are true. When our roots grow deep into the Word of God and His promises, we have the eternal hope and strength of God within us. Unbelievers cannot experience this eternal hope, according to the Scriptures:

> For what hope has the godless when he is cut off, when God takes away his life?
>
> —JOB 27:8

Apart from the resurrection of Jesus Christ, there is no hope for mankind. We are hopeless as human beings. When we accept God's salvation, when He changes our heart, we have a genuine hope—a hope that looks to God, not to the world.

Paul, in a written greeting to Timothy, his friend and partner on some missionary journeys, reminds him of "Christ Jesus our hope" (1 Timothy 1:1). Paul encourages Timothy, and each of us, that it is Christ who will help us in life's situations. He will see us through. He is the embodiment and the personification of hope.

When we have Christ active in our lives, we have genuine hope. After all, we live in the eternal hope of God's future grace. And He is with us now and forever! That is our message to the world:

> Always be prepared to give an answer to everyone who asks you to give the reason for the hope that you have.
>
> —1 PETER 3:15

Our hope is in Christ for our salvation, for our eternity. We are indeed lost if the present time is all we have hope in, all we have hope for. But when Christ, and Christ alone, is our hope, we have hope for all eternity.

When we become weary and discouraged, we need to remember that only through God do we have hope, as we declare with the psalmist:

> Why are you downcast, O my soul? Why so disturbed within me? Put your hope in God, for I will yet praise him, my Savior and my God.
>
> —PSALM 42:5

Hope in God is where we must learn to center our minds. We need to constantly remind ourselves, in times of discouragement, to hope in God. When we preach the Word or quote the Word to ourselves, we receive the positive reassurance of life—hope!

We know that God is with us. We are focused on His grace, which is with us now and for eternity. We can keep looking for Jesus in all the circumstances in our lives and in seeking His plan for us. He is the source of our hope:

> May our Lord Jesus Christ himself and God our Father,
> who loved us and by his grace gave us eternal encour-
> agement and good hope, encourage your hearts and
> strengthen you in every good deed and word.
>
> —2 THESSALONIANS 2:16–17

C. S. Lewis believed that when we look first at God, we find joy and peace, hope and love. Those imaginations allow us to run with abandon every day. Praise God from whom all these imaginations flow!

CHAPTER 23

Love

I have adopted a maxim since I broke my leg: "You can't trust anyone unless they have a limp." Though it helps me to laugh about my limp, in a sense, there is a real truth in that statement. I think most of us are inclined to trust people who seem flawed like we are—people who limp.

All of us are limping spiritually. No one lives without a wounded and handicapped heart. None of us is perfect and flawless. We all have scars that we try to hide or cover up; we have hearts that are often reluctant to trust—or to love.

It is a choice to continue to walk around in this life nursing our wounds, being afraid to completely love and trust others. We can continue to be worried and bitter, angry and resentful, critical and judgmental. Or we can seek healing in the person of Jesus Christ. Jesus came to bring healing, as the prophet declares:

> By his wounds we are healed.
>
> —ISAIAH 53:5

Jesus Christ, who was crucified for us, transforms our heart when we believe in Him. His love for us is so great that He died so we may live. He gave up everything so we might fear nothing. His death and resurrection give us a new vision, a new hope, a new world, and a new life. The Scriptures confirm this wonderful reality:

> This is how God showed his love among us: He sent his one and only Son into the world that we might live

177

through him. This is love: not that we loved God, but
that he loved us and sent his Son as an atoning sacrifice
for our sins.

—1 JOHN 4:9–10

It remains for us to choose how we respond to God's love.
We can reject it and continue to live with a wounded heart. Or
we can let the imaginations of God's love fill our hearts and
engulf our lives. God's Word instructs us regarding the path we
should choose:

Love the LORD your God with all your heart and with all
your soul and with all your strength.

—DEUTERONOMY 6:5

This verse tells us how much we should love God. Our love
should not be merely an intellectual response. Remember the
"quickening" that John Wesley experienced? He was transformed
when he experienced love in his heart as well as in his head.

We cannot choose to love God only when it is convenient,
when it fits into our schedule or timetable. We must respond
with a total commitment to loving Him in all the aspects of our
life. We must be abandoned to God in love. Only then, when we
surrender completely to God's love, will we receive emotional
wholeness, as the apostle Paul described it:

And I pray that you, being rooted and established in
love, may have power, together with all the saints, to
grasp how wide and long and high and deep is the love
of Christ, and to know this love that surpasses knowledge—that you may be filled to the measure of all the
fullness of God.

—EPHESIANS 3:17–19

Paul's beautiful description helps me imagine God's love—a
love that is incomprehensible in its *depth* and *width* and *length*

and *height*. Christ's love is beyond measure. Let's consider these limitless dimensions of God's love.

Its *depth* is demonstrated by how far down He reached to save each of us. The story of the wicked king, Manasseh, in the Old Testament gives us just one example of God's great mercy. Manasseh became king at age twelve and grew to be a detestable king. He restored all the practices of idolatry that his father, Hezekiah, had abolished. Finally, he was captured by the Assyrians, who carried him prisoner to Babylon. Finally, he turned to God:

> In his distress he sought the favor of the LORD his God and humbled himself greatly before the God of his fathers. And when he prayed to him, the LORD was moved by his entreaty and listened to his plea; so he brought him back to Jerusalem and to his kingdom. Then Manasseh knew that the LORD is God.
>
> —2 CHRONICLES 33:12–13

God reached down to save Manasseh at the lowest point in his life, after he had committed reprehensible sins against God. He will reach down to us, no matter how far away from Him we feel.

Hear how *wide* Christ's love is, how it extends to all people:

> With your blood you purchased men for God from every tribe and language and people and nation.
>
> —REVELATION 5:9

The *length* of Christ's love may be described by the fact that He never leaves us or forsakes us, walking through all our trials with us, supporting and upholding us:

> We are hard pressed on every side, but not crushed; perplexed, but not in despair; persecuted, but not abandoned; struck down, but not destroyed. We always carry

around in our body the death of Jesus, so that the life of Jesus may also be revealed in our body.

—2 CORINTHIANS 4:8–10

The *height* of Christ's love can be represented by the exalted position to which He brings us—to the right hand of God, to the throne of God, to intimacy with Him as His bride forever in heaven. The Scriptures declare this reality:

But you have come to Mount Zion, to the heavenly Jerusalem, the city of the living God. You have come to thousands upon thousands of angels in joyful assembly, to the church of the firstborn, whose names are written in heaven. You have come to God, the judge of all men, to the spirits of righteous men made perfect, to Jesus the mediator of a new covenant, and to the sprinkled blood that speaks a better word than the blood of Abel.

—HEBREWS 12:22–24

We should stand in awe of the immeasurable love of Christ! The Christ who redeems us. The Christ who saves us. The Christ who lives in us and transforms us. This reality should motivate us to focus our imaginations on how much He loves us and how much we love Him. We should seek a life filled with constant imaginations of "this love that surpasses knowledge." Our response to God's love should be to choose to live a life of love:

Be imitators of God, therefore, as dearly loved children and live a life of love, just as Christ loved us and gave himself up for us as a fragrant offering and sacrifice to God.

—EPHESIANS 5:1

According to the Scriptures, the love that God gives us we are to give to others. A life of love is not love directed merely toward God. Instead, we must direct God's love, as it flows through us, to others:

> Dear friends, let us love one another, for love comes
> from God. Everyone who loves has been born of God
> and knows God. Whoever does not love does not know
> God, because God is love. If anyone says, "I love God,"
> yet hates his brother, he is a liar. For anyone who does
> not love his brother, whom he has seen, cannot love God,
> whom he has not seen. And he has given us this com-
> mand: whoever loves God must also love his brother.
> —1 JOHN 4:7–8, 20–21

I think loving others gives us an inward glow and makes us
truly beautiful. I saw two sisters the other day conversing with
another person and teasing each other. The first sister said of the
second, "She's the pretty one." The second one replied, "Oh, no.
She's the pretty one." Both sisters are beautiful—inside and out.
Their inner glow enhances their physical beauty.

Letting love spread is an essential imagination of the mind.
Loving others isn't always easy. Author C. S. Lewis decided that to
love is to take a risk, to be vulnerable, to reveal oneself to another
being. With our wounded human hearts, we may be reluctant to
take that risk. On the other hand, to be totally secure and without
risk means loving nothing and no one. If we risk little, we lose
little. But we also gain little out of life. Hear the words of Jesus as
He quotes the prophecy of Isaiah:

> "For this people's heart has become calloused; they
> hardly hear with their ears, and they have closed their
> eyes. Otherwise they might see with their eyes, hear with
> their ears, understand with their hearts and turn, and I
> would heal them."
> —MATTHEW 13:15

God has shown us a better way. He has taken the risk for us.
He loved us so much that He let His Son die on the cross for us.
He has given with complete abandon. And He is ready to heal

us. No longer will we be people who limp! We are perfected through His grace.

And He wants us to have the same loving, giving attitude as Christ: to give in an abandoned way to all people. He doesn't want us to love others with a selfish motive. God's love is not self-serving. He wants us to accept the risks associated with loving, committing those risks to Him. He will take care of the sufferings that may occur because we love and care for others. He wants us to love without fear of the consequences:

> There is no fear in love. But perfect love drives out fear.
> —1 JOHN 4:18

God's love is complete and pure; it is perfect. It is the love that drives out the fear of rejection and humiliation we associate with the risk of loving others. We don't need to guard against being hurt, thereby setting limits on our ability to love.

Instead, we can love with abandon, casting all our cares and anxieties on Him, freeing us to love others even more. This is the love that satisfies. This is the love that fulfills. This is the love that transforms. This is the love God demonstrated for us through the sacrifice of His Son. May we share His gift through our love for Him and for others.

CHAPTER 24

The Strong Foundation

Are you a jealous or envious person? Or can you rejoice in a
brother's success? Do you always desire to get even? Or do you
pray for the total forgiveness of those who have hurt you? Are you
more concerned about helping yourself than helping others? Or
do you find satisfaction in giving generously to others' needs? All
these attitudes reflect a central question: who do you love above
all—Christ or yourself?

The Old Testament tells us the story of the relationship between
two friends—David and Jonathan. These two men reflected the
perfect harmony of the attributes of God in their friendship.
Their love produced grace; that grace produced mercy; and that
mercy produced forgiveness.

Jonathan did not share his father's prejudices against David.
And David did not hold it against Jonathan that he was loyal to
his father, even though Saul was opposing David and threatening
his life. (See 1 Samuel 20.) They knew each other and knew each
other's heart. Most of all, they both knew the heart of God.

Like David and Jonathan, we will find such peace in relationships only when we cultivate an abandoned and loving relationship
with the Lord; then we will be able to share His love with others.

Jesus needs to be the strong foundation in every relationship.
With Him as the foundation of our relationships, we will be people who intercede for others. For example, in a marriage relationship, each person must work to give and forgive, praying for his
or her spouse; otherwise selfishness will destroy the relationship.
We are intercessors when we live responsively to God's Spirit.

Relationships are critical to success in life! I see people who achieve so much and accomplish so much, but who forget to cultivate good relationships with others. They may have some superficial relationships, but they have none with real substance. This sad reality robs them of life, because relationships are what make life so rich and rewarding.

Let me tell you about a doctor who formerly worked at St. Luke's. He specialized in relationships. He made patients feel great and special. He had this little smile and twinkle about him that gave a lift to everyone. He may not have realized the kind of worldly success others achieve; but he did well. He was even named president of the Pennsylvania Ophthalmological Society.

More importantly, he knew that monetary rewards would never be completely satisfying. And he knew that people who look only for worldly success will never be happy. But doctors who view their practice of medicine from the perspective of how much good they can do for their patients have a different kind of success found in true satisfaction. That is the satisfaction which he had!

I think it is easy for people who love Christ to love others. They build strong relationships with people because they have open hearts and are willing to trust others. But those who have trouble loving people will struggle to love Christ. Relationships don't come easily to them, and it is difficult to trust and surrender to the Lord if it is difficult to trust others.

We need to surrender to God's love, His grace, His mercy, His forgiveness in our lives every day, and express these godly attributes to others. We cannot allow ourselves to be spiritual "couch potatoes" who receive life and love from the Holy Spirit but never give back to others. We want to have all the spiritual strength there is by loving others, showing grace and forgiveness and mercy.

STORGE

Many people think of romantic love just as a sexual relationship. If there isn't a sexual relationship, or that aspect has diminished, they conclude that love is absent. There is one essential ingredient that makes the difference between love relationships that are lasting and those that are fleeting—that ingredient is *affection*.

C. S. Lewis, in his book, *The Four Loves*, discusses the nuances of four Greek words that define love. *Storge* (pronounced stor-gay), also referred to as "family love", is a Greek word for love that involves a kind of affection that includes respect, caring for, encouragement, but especially appreciation.[1] *Storge* is a kind of affection that mingles with the other three kinds of love described in the Greek language—friendship (*phileo*), erotic love (*eros*), and the love of God (*agapeo*). Imaginations of appreciation (*storge*), strengthen all our love relationships.

Storge—affection, encouragement, appreciation for others—is an essential part of all true love relationships. Having the mindset of *storge*, as C. S. Lewis says, is so important. Without it, we lose the joy and the spirit that God wants us to have in our relationships. All the relationships of life that are void of *storge* are not loves, but are "un-loves."

Where appreciation is present, we are interested in more than experiencing a sexual relationship. When one's spouse is appreciated and respected, the focus is on giving to that spouse rather than on getting something in return. When this affection becomes paramount in a marriage relationship, then *eros* becomes true love.

Erotic love without appreciation is just the opposite of love; it is selfishness and greed. We enter a sexual relationship to get something for ourselves—a sense of security or a source for sexual gratification. But when appreciation combines with *eros*, then true love grows.

There is a story about a great trader who lived on a faraway island. The time came in his life when he was ready to get married and settle down. The custom in that part of the world was for men to choose a wife and pay the family a dowry. The size of the dowry depended on how much the girl was worth. A beautiful girl was worth five or six cows. An unattractive girl was worth just one cow.

The trader could choose any girl he wanted to be his wife. Finally he decided and approached the girl's father. Now, most people, including the father, knew the girl was really only worth one cow. But the trader saw special qualities in her. He saw she was a radiant person with great potential. He offered her father a dowry of eight cows! The father accepted, thinking that he had gotten quite a bargain.

During the first five years of their marriage, the trader encouraged his wife continually, nurturing the special qualities he saw in her. He appreciated her, reassured her, and loved her. As a result, the woman became one of the most remarkable on the island.

The father observed the change in his daughter and accused the trader: "You cheated me. You didn't give me enough cattle for my daughter. She is worth ten cows, at least." The father finally realized the true value of his daughter.

The young couple watched her father and smiled at each other. Instinctively, they understood that their relationship, built on appreciating and encouraging each other—*storge*—was what made each of them special.

That is a picture of what *storge* is all about. We appreciate, care, support, encourage, and have affection for others, which allows them to live up to their full potential. The Scripture declares:

> If we love one another, God lives in us and his love is made complete in us.
>
> —1 JOHN 4:12

Appreciation transforms our relationship with others and gives it greater meaning. *Storge* is a selfless love interested in the good of others. We no longer worry about ourselves. We treat others with dignity and respect. *Storge* sees the good in others and dwells on the positive. We anticipate the other person's desires and interests and we seek to meet those needs in deference.

Storge also transforms our relationship with God. No longer do we have a formal relationship with lip service, but we have a vital, deeply personal and intimate relationship with Him. We have a constant appreciation for God, valuing and esteeming Him above all else. We see Him as incomparable. We appreciate Jesus so much that we do not seek the appreciation of other human beings. At the same time, we abandon ourselves to God, relinquishing everything to Him. *Storge* focuses on God's glory—praising, worshiping, and adoring Him.

Storge is often misunderstood. Some people have never received unconditional love and they do not think they are worthy. Some people think they have to do something to earn another person's approval. Some people have trouble showing affection. They think they have to give something extra to others. They cannot just be themselves and relax. Others may give their bodies in erotic relationships to overcome their feelings of inadequacy.

Affection is one of our basic needs. God calls us to be His friends, not just His servants. The affection He feels for us is something we must feel deeply. God loves us and has made everything possible for us. When we feel His affection, we can pass that love on to others. It gives us an enduring life because when we are full of appreciation, we are filled with love and kindness. *Storge* gets rid of worry and bitterness and a critical spirit toward others. We are no longer determined to find the bad in situations and people. When we focus on *storge*, our relationships are fueled by the eternal fire of God's love. We respect others, we encourage others, we appreciate others, and we love others.

MARRIAGE

For those readers who are married, let me challenge you to be honest with yourself. What do *you* think about your relationship with your spouse? Answer yourself honestly. Not what you tell other people, even your spouse, but what you really think. Is it a good relationship or a bad one? Would you marry your spouse again or would you rather not be married to your partner? Are you feelings growing positively or negatively?

Let's consider the marriage relationship briefly, which I believe is the most dominant relationship of life. While other relationships are formed on a foundation of friendship, commitment, appreciation, and godly love, marriage not only contains those elements, but also leads to sex.

For followers of Christ, love between a man and a woman should be centered in Christ's love for them. The agape love of Christ was shown for each of them, and each of them should show that love toward the other. This concept of love is foreign to many people. How blessed is the couple that has surrendered their hearts to Christ!

Do you look at your spouse as God's gift to you? Do you look at God first or your spouse first? The role you give Jesus in your marriage relationship says much about the role He has in the rest of your relationships, indeed, in the rest of your life.

When I wake up every morning, I ask Jesus to be revealed in every area of my wife's life. I ask God's blessings for Heather each day, blessing her with the presence of Jesus in her mind and her eyes and her heart, so that she thinks and sees and loves as Jesus does.

Respect, godly character, friendship, affection, and enjoyment are the basis of a good marriage. Two people who marry should understand each other, love each other, and care for each other. In marriage, as in all relationships, we can be truly happy if we are thankful and have an appreciative heart for one another.

There is one more area of imaginations that is especially critical to the health of a marriage and that is the area of mental fantasies.

Many married people struggle with romantic fantasies about other people. Some may act on those fantasies and pursue relationships outside their marriage. Or the fantasies may remain fantasies, while the person stays true to his or her spouse, but cause a sense of guilt or condemnation for them. Others may use their fantasies to generate excitement within their own marriage, pretending their spouse is the person about whom they fantasize. And still others may try to deny, even to themselves, that they have fantasies.

All of us have fantasies. Some writers have said that men struggle with them more than women do, but I think all of us face this problem to a greater or lesser extent. None of us is perfect when it comes to our own intimacy. We cannot ignore fantasies and hope that they go away. We must be honest and admit our weaknesses. If we truly want to have a Christlike mind, we have to deal with our fantasies in a way that will glorify God.

First, we should not be surprised that believers struggle with fantasies. However, we are still under the provision of God's grace because we have faith in Him through Jesus Christ. We must continue to look to Him for our deliverance from sin:

> Therefore, there is now no condemnation for those who are in Christ Jesus, because through Christ Jesus the law of the Spirit of life set me free from the law of sin and death.
>
> —ROMANS 8:1–2

Second, we must remember we are not alone in temptation. God has given us the Holy Spirit to guide us, even as we deal with fantasies. The Holy Spirit can empower each of us to direct the fantasies toward one's spouse. The Holy Spirit can strengthen us when we feel tempted.

We can do more than simply say, "I'm not going to give in." We can relinquish our struggle and let the Holy Spirit guide us and protect us. And we can let that desire be filled and complemented with a desire for God—a desire to love God, to be committed to God, to know God. The best plan is to find God in everything, and to even make our intimacy part of our relationship with Him. Then we can let that desire strengthen our marriage.

I think part of the problem is that frequently we take sex too seriously and marriage not seriously enough. The priority here is that we make marriage a lot of fun, but also recognize its great importance and significance.

Now, this does not mean that sex should be solemn and serious. In a committed, Christian relationship, sex should be a joyous time when two people are intimate together: they can talk, they can pray, they can enjoy being themselves.

Some people are so serious that they cannot be affectionate. Some people are so serious they cannot laugh and enjoy each other. Sex is a joyous gift from God that should be enjoyed. It can, and should, include laughter that does not degrade, but simply relaxes and promotes enjoyment. As a married couple, we should laugh and rejoice in our sexual relationship with each other as our lives are surrendered to Christ.

CHAPTER 25

Loving Jesus, Loving Others

Let's face it, in any relationship we will struggle with ways to resolve conflicts. As we have discussed, only when we are focused on Jesus, can we be truly loving. We can put the other person first, we can listen, we can be humble, and we can give. While it is unrealistic to believe that conflict will ever be eliminated, as we focus on Christ, we will have the tools to resolve problems rather than letting them fester and destroy the relationship.

Without Jesus, we put ourselves first, which is a selfish attitude that will eventually destroy our relationship. Here are some ways that happens:

- We seek recognition from other people rather than finding contentment in serving God.

I know people who will go out of their way to be recognized for something they did that has no real meaning. There are others who desire success so desperately that they will even adopt bad business practices, such as altering their books, so that they will appear successful. They deceive others in order to feel better about themselves.

- We blame others for our own problems.

Some people who have trouble with their hearing won't admit their problem. Instead, they blame others for speaking too quickly or too slowly, too loudly or too softly. Others, who may be unhappy within a marriage, seek to blame the problems in their relationship on the spouse. So they look for other relationships, thinking a different person will make them happy.

- We want to control a relationship and make the other person give us what we want.

There are many reasons for becoming a controlling person. By controlling, we feel more important and powerful, trying to manipulate another. Frequently the relationship disintegrates because the controlling nature of one person prevents a truly balanced, loving relationship from forming. Unhappily, the one thing the controlling person wanted—a relationship—fails to materialize.

There is a better way to guide someone with whom you want to establish a relationship. It is the Socratic way of asking questions, which imparts knowledge without being controlling or manipulative. We can ask such questions as, "What are the consequences of your behavior?" The answers to our questions determine the best decision to a situation. This approach is the opposite of trying to control another's thoughts and actions. Though it takes time, tenderness, and imagination, it is a great way to guide a child, or friends, or others in personal and business relationships.

If we are not careful, we find it easy to blame others for our own shortcomings. Or we prize the love and approval of others more than we should. If our life is characterized either by seeking others' approval or blaming others, we have not found true contentment in Christ.

Underneath these attitudes is the belief that says we do not need God. We are good all on our own. In our selfishness, we become self-righteous, not relying on the power of God's Spirit. We disapprove of the sin—and the sinner.

We can see the underlying attitude that "we don't need God" by the way we treat others. Saul of Tarsus exemplified this attitude of self-reliance. He hated Stephen, a man full of faith and the Holy Spirit. Acts 8:1 records that Saul gave approval to Stephen's death. Saul was a very harsh, uncaring man toward Christians.

He was self-righteous and didn't think he needed God's grace. Later, after a powerful encounter with Jesus, Saul was humbled and converted, becoming the great apostle Paul.

In contrast to Saul's cruel self-righteousness, in the Lord Jesus we constantly see love for others, particularly the sinner—even Saul. When Jesus walked the earth, He surprised the self-righteous Pharisees by his direct, clear love for sinners as the following story reveals:

> When Jesus reached the spot, he looked up and said to him, "Zacchaeus, come down immediately. I must stay at your house today." So he came down at once and welcomed him gladly. All the people saw this and began to mutter, "He has gone to be the guest of a 'sinner.'"
>
> —LUKE 19:5–7

Zacchaeus was a notorious swindler in the community—a traitor to the Jews, working for the Romans to take taxes from his own Jewish people. When he climbed a tree to see Jesus pass by, Jesus looked up and told him He was going to his house, completely shocking the Pharisees with the idea that He would be the guest in a sinner's home.

How evident is the Lord Jesus' beautiful spirit toward sinners. He is compassionate and interested. He truly is the model for all our relationships.

While we must hate sin, as God does, we are called to love the sinner, as He does as well. We are called to pray for the sinner, including our own sinful ways. We are called to intercede for others—to pray fervently for each other.

Now, it is not always easy to be a loving intercessor. There are times when others are difficult to deal with. They may be filled with anger or worry or cynicism, or other negative attitudes. But our godly response is to love them and pray for them. We need to be continually filled with the Holy Spirit, praying even for those who "use" us, hate us, and act against us.

The Reverend Larry Jackson from North Carolina teaches that we must pray from the position of the person for whom we are interceding. We use our imaginations to put ourselves in that person's position. If that person is in a state of disarray, we must imagine their anguish and pray for them. From that compassionate position, we often find ourselves awake to God, feeling the turmoil and grief of the person as we pray for him or her. Each of us has gifts from God. How do we use these gifts in our relationships? Do we use them to build up others in a spirit of intercession and righteous truth, or do we use them to build up ourselves, by criticizing, judging, admonishing, condemning, or telling others what to do? Do we seek the truth at all costs, or do we temper our actions and thoughts with our imaginations of a loving God? Are we critical of others, admonishing and correcting them? Or do we build others up, appreciating and thanking them?

It is easy to delude ourselves, denying our struggles. We rationalize, we lie, and we say all sorts of things that are misleading, especially to ourselves. That is why it is essential to be brutally honest with ourselves, admitting our struggles.

We also need to learn to be accountable to other people of the same sex. We must take the next step and admit our struggles to someone else. God made us to share each others' burdens. Our load becomes lighter when it is shared.

The principle of accountability and being responsible is a great help to keep focused on a desire to honor God and to say, "Thy will be done," even when something is unpleasant to us.

For example, if one of your children opens the car door in a parking lot, damaging a gold Porsche parked in the next slot, it would be responsible to go to all lengths to find the owner of the Porsche to make the situation right. You may not do this with overflowing joy, but you do what is right from a desire to honor God. Along with that action comes peace and a sweetness from submitting to God's difficult providences and doing what is right.

Being responsible is part of Christian maturity, which is demonstrated in very practical circumstances, such as picking up trash scattered from one's curbside garbage can during the night by the neighborhood cat! We probably aren't elated with a sense of privilege, but we do what is right out of a desire to honor God.

God knows how to bless those actions. He knows how to give a peace and sweetness to our decision to say, "Thy will be done." Becoming responsible is another motivation for living righteously that God uses to direct us through unpleasant circumstances.

Before long we discover God uses these occasions in positive ways that surprise us. Then we will thank Him for the circumstances and rejoice to have such an overruling God in all the details of our life. Ultimately it comes back to a desire to honor the Lord Jesus in any situation.

Our hearts must be continually turned to God so that we become pliable through His love; then we can love others. When we focus our thoughts on the person of Jesus we will not be accusers of others; we are filled with love and compassion for them. Let's focus on Jesus Christ so others can see Christ in us.

CHAPTER 26

Delusion of Reprieve

How often have you procrastinated in dealing with negative consequences of your actions, hoping the problem will sort itself out or just go away? There is a false imagination at work here—a delusion that Satan uses to keep us separated from God. I call it a "delusion of reprieve," which makes us hope that God will just smooth problems over, that He won't hold us accountable for our thoughts and actions.

How very wrong this thinking is! Yet we may all have times in our life in which we hope God will give us a reprieve from the consequences of our actions. For example, I have walked into a classroom to take an exam, having been involved in activities other than studying the night before the test. Then I would ask God to give me wisdom, knowledge, and discernment for taking the exam. Unfortunately, I did not do well on the test. I wonder why! Was my faith insufficient? God could have made me smart even though I had not studied the material. But He did not. Instead, He held me accountable for my actions.

I am accountable to God for the way I treat anyone with whom I do business. I must always ask myself how the Lord would treat that person if He were in my shoes. As Director of St. Luke's Cataract and Laser Institute, I am accountable for more than three hundred employees. If I hurt those people in such a way that would influence them to turn away from the Lord, I am held accountable. I am responsible for everyone who works for me.

I am also accountable for my thoughts. It is not enough for my actions to honor and worship and obey God. For each of us, as we have discussed, our thoughts must also be focused on Him. We must let His mind become our minds. To think we can allow lustful thoughts if we don't commit adultery is a delusion. It is a delusion to think these thoughts are OK. Jesus taught that our lustful imaginations are just as wrong as the actions of adultery:

> "You have heard that it was said, 'Do not commit adultery.' But I tell you that anyone who looks at a woman lustfully has already committed adultery with her in his heart."
>
> —MATTHEW 5:27–28

One of my friends graciously confronted a gentleman who went to church but who was living a lifestyle of disobedience to Christ's commands. His response to my friend's correction was: "Oh, don't worry about it. I'm just a carnal Christian."

This gentleman had the imagination of himself as someone who was saved, but who was simply not living under the lordship of Jesus Christ. He accepted God's grace, but was indifferent to his responsibilities for living a life in Christ. He wasn't living under the premise that God is sovereign. His mind-set was preventing the Holy Spirit from abounding in him. This gentleman needed to ask himself, "Does Christ really mean anything to me?"

How often are we indifferent to our responsibilities in living a life for Christ? Are there times when we think He will forgive us and we'll be OK, regardless of how we live?

Now, certainly, we trust in God's grace—the power of His resurrection over our sins and every area affected by our sins. We know that God is sovereign and we can trust in Him to meet our daily needs. But the fact that the Lord forgave us for our sins does not mean we do not have to go to work in the morning to provide food for our family.

We must guard against a delusion of misunderstanding God's grace. The wrong attitude is saying: "I don't have to worry about anything; God will take care of everything." "I don't have to worry about creating bad debts because God will take care of me." "I don't' have to worry about not taking care of my physical health because His grace will take care of me." "I don't have to worry about being spiritually and ethically correct, because God's grace will cover all my sins."

Grace does indeed cover the sins of those who have a living trust in Christ. Praise God that He is so merciful to us! But His grace doesn't excuse us from living in a way that responds in obedience to Him. Grace is not a license for sin. We need to be fiscally responsible. We need to be responsible for our physical bodies, making sure we are living a healthy lifestyle. We need to be responsible for our minds, staying mentally sharp. And we need to be responsible in all our thoughts and actions, which should be aligned to fulfill the will of God for our lives.

We cannot intentionally continue to sin and rely on a faulty assumption that our sin will be covered by God's grace. If we do, in essence, we are lying to ourselves. We are trying to convince ourselves that God doesn't need to be in control of every area of our lives. John Owen, who is considered by many to be one of the greatest Puritan theologians, wanted those who heard him to, "Be sure of this and let it be fixed in your mind, that if you do not repent of this secret sin you are engaged in, you will perish forever."

Owen, like many Reformed theologians, believed wholeheartedly in God's sovereignty in salvation. God's grace is indeed sufficient for all our sins. But Owen also emphasized our human responsibility to live out our faith with a transformed heart and mind.

Let's consider again the example of adultery. If someone who claimed to be a Christian was living in adultery, there are those who would say that sinful lifestyle cannot hinder their salvation; they were saved when they "made their decision for Christ" and they can never be lost, even though they may ruin their family. Some use the expression, "once saved, always saved," to support this opinion.

This is an incomplete teaching. We are saved by the blood of Christ AND a changed heart that continues to fight the fight of faith to the end, as the Scriptures clearly teach:

> Therefore, if anyone is in Christ, he is a new creation; the old has gone, the new has come!
>
> —2 Corinthians 5:17

Just because someone makes a "decision for Christ" doesn't mean they have experienced a saving change in their heart. Our life must back up our words. It is a Christian's joy to be firmly trusting in the heart of God, engulfed in the Trinity, interwoven with the person of Christ, living in His pure and perfect love and grace. Grace is such a beautiful, supernatural aspect of our life. It is a shame to cheapen it by not putting Christ in everything we do or not totally abiding in Him to live righteous lives.

Unfortunately, at times we may be unwatchful and "play" with sin, biting on Satan's lures. We can get complacent. We think we can sin just this one time because we have been faithful in the past. In those seasons of temptation, we need to hear God's Word:

> So, if you think you are standing firm, be careful that you don't fall!
>
> —1 Corinthians 10:12

At other times, we may feel weak in our faith and sense that sin is greater than we are. God does not let us struggle alone, as Paul continues to exhort believers:

> No temptation has seized you except what is common to man. And God is faithful; he will not let you be tempted beyond what you can bear. But when you are tempted, he will also provide a way out so that you can stand up under it.
>
> —1 Corinthians 10:13

As our Father and Savior, God will help us. This verse points out the perfect balance of grace and responsibility. God's sovereign faithfulness will provide strength to obey, and we must continue to repent and believe in His grace.

We cannot assume that our profession of faith is a guarantee that we are saved and always will be. Every day we must persevere in the fight of faith.

Jonathan Edwards explained it this way: "That there is a real difference between them that fall away and them that persevere... [they fall away] because they have no root in themselves; because they have not counted the cost; and because they have no oil in their vessels. Those who have no root differ from those who have root. Those who have oil differ from those who have no oil."

The Bible teaches that those who enter heaven must persevere in the fight of faith. Jesus declared: "He who stands firm to the end will be saved (Matthew 10:22). And the apostle Paul warned Timothy that we must "fight the good fight of faith" (1 Timothy 6:12). Our responsibility is to continue in faith, for without faith there is no relationship with the person of Jesus Christ.

According to the Scriptures, you will only be presented as a righteous saint in heaven by Christ, "if you continue in your faith, established and firm, not moved from the hope held out in the gospel" (Colossians 1:23). And Jesus taught that in order to persevere, we must take action against sin:

> If your right hand causes you to sin, cut it off and throw it away. It is better for you to lose one part of your body than for your whole body to go into hell.
> —MATTHEW 5:30

Sin destroys our claim to having true faith. Sin is contrary to the principle of faith. When we are flirting with temptation, we must remember God's promise in Deuteronomy, which is repeated in the Book of Hebrews:

"Never will I leave you; never will I forsake you."
—HEBREWS 13:5

God vows to be with us and to provide the divine help we need to overcome temptation. He is behind the scenes to revive our faith and hear our call for help, bringing us to repentance. Consider these divine promises for the penitent believer:

Though he stumble, he will not fall, for the LORD upholds him with his hand.
—PSALM 37:24

But the Lord is faithful, and he will strengthen and protect you from the evil one.
—2 THESSALONIANS 3:3

Remember, these promises are made to those who believe. If there is no faith, we cannot claim the promise. True faith resulting in true salvation is to be forgiven and to become a new creature in Christ—revealed through a transformed life of faith. We must have a saving union with Christ that makes a difference in the way we live our life.

If we imagine that He won't hold us accountable for our thoughts and actions, we begin to think, "Maybe I don't need God." I can be independent and do what I want because it doesn't matter to God. We no longer live by faith. We no longer live according to the mind of Christ.

Dr. James D. Smith often teaches on "the laboratory of the mind," claiming that when there is a sin in our lives, we have told ourselves the Lord doesn't care about this area of our lives. This is an imagining by the mind that is a lie.

Lying to ourselves is so dangerous! We may try to deceive ourselves, but we can never deceive God. He knows our hearts. He knows our thoughts. He knows our minds. Sin will separate us from God. We will never be able to fully focus our imaginations on Him when our lies create a chasm between us.

Have you ever talked and acted a certain way around one group of friends, and then talked and acted differently with another group? Do you talk one way around your golf buddies or when playing bridge, but act differently around the dinner table with your family? While it may be OK to relate differently in various relationships, this kind of behavior becomes dangerous when there is a definite break between who we are in one group and who we become in a second group.

For example, I have known people who love to be with the "in" crowd on Saturday night and then attend worship services on Sunday morning. Sometimes they exhibit a smug attitude in this contradictory behavior that says, "I'm getting away with something while others are living by the rules." The two lifestyles are not integrated. They are kept in separate "boxes" inside a person's mind. They think their behavior doesn't affect anyone. But this is false thinking.

It is a delusion to think we can divide our affections and our actions. In reality, this behavior hurts everyone. In its most extreme form, a delusion of reprieve is the mind-set for nonbelievers, which denies that the Bible is the true authority. They don't believe God will hold them accountable because they do not believe in Him and do not love Him. They think they can get by with living a life outside of Christ.

One of the greatest men I know is a lawyer who lives very reputably; in appearance, everything about him is good. He is tall, good-looking, respected in the community and in his profession. But he does not believe the Bible is the Word of God or that Jesus Christ is the Savior. He thinks all he needs is to demonstrate is good actions. He is probably less "sinful" in his lifestyle than any man I know.

But he will not have a place in God's heaven because, though he may be a great lawyer and a "good" person, these are external appearances. They do not represent a life of faith that results from a relationship with Jesus Christ. Until he really loves Jesus, understanding his need for a Savior, he is suffering under the delusion of reprieve. This man, as good as he is according to man's standards, will go to hell rather than spend eternity with the living God.

What a dangerous attitude! If we don't believe in God and His Word, we are telling God to go His way and we will go ours. When we do not believe that we are sinners in the eyes of God who need a Savior, we are telling God that our independence, our sinful life on earth, is more important than His truth and His eternal life.

There are many people who carry this attitude into their living. Unlike my lawyer friend, they may not even necessarily be seeking to be "good" people. They treat people the way the world treats them. They are not honorable; they are not kind and loving. Instead, they are bitter, angry, resentful, worried, self-centered, and destructive. When they make decisions, they don't consider the eternity beyond the grave. Thus, they make superficial decisions that cost them dearly, taking them farther from the heart of God.

The truth is that we matter to God. More than that, we are His children! He loves us. He cares about our thoughts and actions. He cares about how we choose to think and what we choose to do. We must allow the Holy Spirit to convict us of our sins and then receive the grace of God to forgive us and redeem us from our sins. So often people have a hard time believing they are sinners, which is an example of the delusion of reprieve. Others do not believe that God's grace is great enough to save them. They think they have to earn salvation by doing good works. We can get caught on either one of these points and not really rise to the joy of being saved by His grace.

We must be clear on this point: God, who saves us by His grace, calls us to persevere in the fight of faith by His grace. When we are tempted to walk away from our faith we must ask ourselves whether we choose Christ or choose sin. If we choose sin and do not repent, we will perish.

Our faith is nourished by secret springs that are not known to the world. Every day we must thank God that our faith is sustained by the heavenly intercession of Christ for us (Romans 8:34), who also declared:

> "Because I live, you also will live."
> —JOHN 14:19

In *The Pilgrim's Progress* there is a wonderful image of how Christ sustains our faith. Christian, the parable's hero, is shown a fire in front of a wall. A man is pouring water on it, yet the fire grows higher and hotter. He does not understand why the fire will not go out. Then he is shown the other side of the wall, where he sees another man secretly pouring oil into the fire.

The fire represents the grace of God in our heart. The man with the bucket of water is Satan, trying to drown out our faith. Behind the wall is Christ, who is sustaining the faith of the believer with the oil of the Holy Spirit.

What a powerful image to fix in our minds! We do not need to live in the fear of perishing because of temptation to sin! God supports us and keeps us strong. We live in loving gratitude to Christ for interceding in times of temptation. He will strengthen us. And we are never alone!

CHAPTER 27

A Forgiving Spirit

Have you ever been falsely accused by someone? Has anyone ever hurt you, either intentionally or unknowingly? What should your imaginations be in those circumstances? How does focusing on Jesus affect your attitude?

Consider the death of Christ on the cross. Imagine Him, as He was dying, looking down from the cross at His tormentors. He was exhausted and broken; pain seared His body. Yet, He wasn't hoping for some miracle to save Him. He wasn't angry. He wasn't plotting His revenge. Listen to His words:

> "Father, forgive them, for they do not know what they are doing."
>
> —LUKE 23:34

Jesus, through His death and resurrection, procured God's forgiveness not just for those who plotted against Him and killed Him but for all who have sinned. According to the Scriptures, we are all sinners. We are born into sin that infects all of mankind, and we struggle with sins that result from our own selfishness. If we are honest, we must admit to this sinful state:

> If we claim to be without sin, we deceive ourselves and the truth is not in us.
>
> —1 JOHN 1:8

None of us can deny that we sin. The good news is that God does not leave us in this sinful state. If we confess our sins, he is faithful and just and will forgive us our sins and purify us from all unrighteousness. (See 1 John 1:9.) When we choose to believe in the cleansing blood of Christ's death and resurrection, we can receive forgiveness and be freed from sin. Christianity is the state of forgiveness. God forgives us. He purifies us. He saves us through Jesus Christ:

> Here is a trustworthy saying that deserves full acceptance: Christ Jesus came into the world to save sinners.
> —1 TIMOTHY 1:15

When we are falsely accused, our minds need to focus on Christ's loving sacrifice for us. Jesus, as God, gave up His rights. He died on the cross for us, even though He did not deserve to die and we did not deserve such a loving action. God did not give us what we deserved—eternal death as punishment for sin. He forgave us completely—and died the death we should have died. Through His sacrifice, we received everything—eternal life!

That is the beautiful image of forgiveness I like to hold in my mind: Jesus' forgiveness as the complete, unqualified, unconditional giving of Himself.

Yet, receiving and believing in His forgiveness is only one side of the coin. When we experience His limitless forgiveness of our sins, we are able to forgive others. We act out His forgiveness of our sins by forgiving others. My satisfaction in His perfect forgiveness allows me to be forgiving in relationships with others.

Let me give you an example. Let's say a friend says something unfair to me. So I replay the events in my head and get angry. Instead of recognizing this vain imagination, I nurse my bad feelings. Instead of focusing on Jesus' forgiveness to save me and extending that forgiveness to my friend, I begin to savor my anger. I let thoughts of revenge and retaliation fill my mind. I start to feel tense and stressed out, reaching exhaustion.

Soon, Satan has a stronghold in my mind; I am filled with death, not Christ's overflowing life. My entire perspective is distorted and I become useless to the Lord. I cannot function as a man of God, for I am filled with sin-filled imaginations because of my inability to forgive.

I could have changed that scenario. And I should have. I should have asked God for help to forgive. I should have thanked Jesus for His sacrificial forgiveness and the power to channel that forgiveness to my offender. I should have prayed for deliverance from the evil thoughts. I should have meditated on God's love for me and His promise to never leave me or forsake me. I should have, I should have, I should have.

It is up to me to choose what thoughts fill my mind. I choose my own attitude. Do I choose anger, resentment, and bitterness? Do I let my desire for revenge distort my thinking and, as a result, spread lies and malicious gossip? Or do I choose forgiveness, as I have been forgiven? God's Word is explicit in its instruction regarding these choices:

> Get rid of all bitterness, rage and anger, brawling and slander, along with every form of malice. Be kind and compassionate to one another, forgiving each other, just as in Christ God forgave you.
> —EPHESIANS 4:31–32

The Lord is gracious to us, and we need to be gracious in return. Forgiveness is to the spirit what exercise is to the physical body. We are given a body, and if we do not exercise it, we become "couch potatoes," weak and unfit for the rigors of life. In that same way, we are given Jesus Christ and His forgiveness, and if we do not forgive others, we become spiritual "couch potatoes." It is our choice. Either we choose to be captives to bitterness and anger because we do not forgive others, or we can demonstrate the forgiveness of Christ to those who offend us.

Jesus taught us to pray: "Forgive us our debts, as we also have forgiven our debtors" (Matthew 6:12). Why should we ask such a thing? Jesus explains:

> "For if you forgive men when they sin against you ,
> your heavenly Father will also forgive you. But if you
> do not forgive men their sins, your Father will not for-
> give your sins."
>
> —MATTHEW 6:14–15

What a serious consequence of harboring unforgiveness! We cannot receive the Father's forgiveness if we do not forgive others. Jesus tells a parable that illustrates this point. He said the "kingdom of heaven is like a king who wanted to settle accounts with his servants" (Matthew 18:23). One servant, who owed the king a great deal of money, was unable to pay his debt. The king ordered that the man and his family be sold to pay the money. But the servant pleaded with the king, and the king forgave his great debt and let the man go.

Yet that servant went to one of his fellow servants who owed him a very small sum of money and demanded to be paid. The servant begged and pleaded: "Be patient with me, and I will pay you back" (v. 29). But the man was unmoved and had the servant thrown into jail. When the master heard about the incident, he called the servant he had forgiven before him.

> "You wicked servant," he said, "I canceled all that debt
> of yours because you begged me to. Shouldn't you have
> had mercy on your fellow servant just as I had on you?"
> In anger his master turned him over to the jailers to be
> tortured, until he should pay back all he owed.
>
> —MATTHEW 18:32–34

Then Jesus tells us clearly the lesson to learn from the parable:

> "This is how my heavenly Father will treat each of you
> unless you forgive your brother from your heart."
>
> —MATTHEW 18:35

Forgiveness is crucial in all our relationships. Otherwise, resentment, bitterness, and anger fester. We build up defensive walls when we deny the hurt and try to convince ourselves that everything is OK. But that only deepens the wound. We damage the dynamic nature of our relationships by running from conflict and pain. Our relationship, especially a marriage or close friendship, will be eventually destroyed because of our lack of forgiveness.

The vain imaginations that stem from an unforgiving heart will also destroy us physically, mentally, emotionally, and spiritually. We are filled with stress, anxiety, and depression. Our blood pressure rises. We can get ulcers and otherwise weaken our physical health. It is not worth the consequences to hold bitterness and resentment in our heart.

All of us have been wronged by others—by lies, by stealing, by gossip, and so on. After all, no one is perfect, not even our friends and loved ones. And when we are wronged, there are times when we would rather respond with anger and resentment than in a forgiving spirit. Let me share an example from my own life.

While growing up near the coal fields in West Virginia, I found out that if I did not do my best, I would be "picked on." While I never proved to be a great competitor or warrior, I acquired the habit of always hitting back. And I always carried a grudge against anyone who did anything against me, always remembering the wrong they did to me.

I reached a point in my life where I was very angry and resentful, returning to anyone who harmed me a "double payback." This negative imagination pulled me down mentally, spiritually, and emotionally, and damaged my ability to enjoy life.

As I began to grow in my relationship with the Lord, I realized how much these negative attitudes were hurting my life, my relationships with others, and my relationship with the Lord. I had to confront my anger and to acknowledge that these attitudes were sinful. I had to choose to repent and let them go.

And then I had to learn to forgive. When I chose to forgive others and let go of my anger, I discovered I was dramatically changed. Forgiveness empowered me to become stronger in my relationship with the Lord. I developed a closer relationship with God, which gave me joy, peace, and inner calm. The Scriptures confirm the negative power of harboring unforgiveness:

> See to it that no one misses the grace of God and that no bitter root grows up to cause trouble and defile many.
> —HEBREWS 12:15

Bitterness, anger, and resentment cause us to trouble and defile our relationship with God and with others. These negative imaginations can only be cured by receiving God's grace and mercy for healing. Then we are truly able to forgive, and, if necessary, to confront hurtful situations in love. Jesus is the source of our forgiveness.

When Christ is the focus of our thoughts, we no longer harbor selfish attitudes that make us unforgiving and judgmental. Our minds are freed from the grudges, bitterness, and anger we experience when we have been wronged.

As human beings, there are limits to our own ability to forgive. But through the love and forgiveness enacted on the cross—Christ's sacrificial and self-emptying love and forgiveness—when we yield our lives to Him, we can learn to love and forgive others. Only through our repentance and focus on Christ can our minds be freed from the bitterness and resentment that keep us from forgiving others.

Forgiveness is an act of unconditional love—one of our greatest images of Christ. When we forgive others, we relinquish our rights as the one sinned against, and we choose to not demand recourse or retaliation. We release our offenders to God. We turn the situation over to Christ, for He is the one who will right all the wrongs. All we can do is pray for those we think have offended us. Our prayers will change us. As I have prayed for my offenders, I have been changed. I have learned that I need to care for others. And I have grown closer to Christ.

When forgiving someone, it is important to be specific—so

specific that we could write down the attitude or event we need to forgive. We cannot generalize specific acts so they become wholesale assaults on character. For example, it is difficult to forgive someone "for being bad."

Instead, we need to forgive what they do, not who they are. We pray for the sinner, but we dislike the sin and refuse to let it become part of our lives. In true forgiveness, we no longer regard the offense as a debt owed to us:

> Do not repay anyone evil for evil. Be careful to do what is right in the eyes of everybody. If it is possible, as far as it depends on you, live at peace with everyone. Do not take revenge, my friends, but leave room for God's wrath, for it is written: "It is mine to avenge; I will repay," says the Lord.
>
> —ROMANS 12:17–19

The world teaches us that the correct response when people hurt us is for us to hurt them back. Unfortunately, when our reaction is mean, angry, or hurtful to others, we are destroyed by our anger and our attempts to hurt others.

God teaches us that the correct response to offense is total forgiveness. The receiver of our forgiveness may not deserve it, according to the imaginations of the world. But God loves that person as He loves us. His forgiveness is free to all who accept it. His response, therefore, should be our response. The greatest measure of forgiveness repays evil with kindness, giving love when there is no reason to love and no guarantee that love will be returned—ever. Jesus taught us the measure of forgiveness:

> Then came Peter to him, and said, Lord, how oft shall my brother sin against me, and I forgive him? till seven times? Jesus saith unto him, I say not unto thee, Until seven times: but, Until seventy times seven.
>
> —MATTHEW 18:21–22, KJV

I am sure Peter thought he was being very generous when he suggested the number seven for forgiving an offender in a day. He probably was overwhelmed when Jesus countered with such a high number. I do not think Jesus intends for us to keep count; His real meaning was that forgiveness should be "countless." He wants us to be people with a forgiving nature who release the offense as often as needed.

One practical way to do this is to say to ourselves, "I forgive this offense (being as specific as possible) in Jesus' name." We can repeat that until it is part of our innermost being. Then we have the power of Christ in us, guiding our forgiveness.

Now, repeated instances of forgiveness should not be confused with tolerance. Forgiveness is not a license for the offender. We must be intolerant of evil. Yet we can still forgive, and let the Lord take care of the rest.

This attitude of forgiveness takes a lot of faith in Christ's love. We have to choose by faith to offer this kind of forgiveness. The apostles responded to Christ's injunction to forgive by saying, "Increase our faith!" (Luke 17:5). We have access to an unlimited source of faith because we have experienced Jesus' sacrificial death of forgiveness. It is His forgiveness that is channeled through us to others. God is in us and works through us.

When we make forgiveness one of the major aspects of our life, we are free from the bondage of resentment and anger. Total forgiveness results in total freedom. A mind-set of forgiveness clears the way so we can focus more fully on Christ. When our thoughts are not cluttered with bitterness and resentment, we are filled with imaginations of joy, peace, and love—blessings we receive from our Lord, Jesus Christ!

CHAPTER 28

A Life of Caring

What do you expect out of your relationships? Is it better to get as much as you can? Or do you try to serve the other person?

Before we can apply any imaginations to our relationships with others, let's look at God's attitude toward us. C. S. Lewis says there is a parallel between creation and redemption. God didn't need to create us. He did it for His own enjoyment, to have a relationship with us. The same is true of redemption. He didn't need to give us Jesus as a Savior. He did it because He wanted to restore the relationship with His people. God's free and giving heart made Him first create us and then later redeem us. It is simply the nature of God—His nature to give and love. Redemption is not based on anything good in us.

While the world seeks to get and be filled, God is already full. He looks forward to giving. He wants to give us His love, His blessings, His riches, so we, in turn, can be channels of giving His abundance to others.

When our minds find satisfaction in God's promises, we find His free and giving heart reflected in our own attitudes. We give to others freely. We are less concerned with what we receive and with having our own needs met. We are not tempted to hoard God's blessings for ourselves. After all, we know that God will satisfy us and always provide for us, according to the measure that we give:

> Remember this: whoever sows sparingly will also reap
> sparingly, and whoever sows generously will also reap
> generously. Each man should give what he has decided

213

in his heart to give, not reluctantly or under compulsion,
for God loves a cheerful giver.

—2 CORINTHIANS 9:6–7

I had an aunt who loved to be pampered. She would stay in bed until ten o'clock every morning. And she spent her days always wanting a little more than she had; she was never satisfied. She had the nicest husband in the world, but I do not think she ever appreciated him. She was consumed with her desire for more. She ended up dissipated and dying. I am not sure she ever found satisfaction from life.

I cannot imagine life without giving. I love to give of myself, not only from financial resources, but also through my profession, and to my community. I never want to retire and just sit around all day. I find the greatest satisfaction in serving others and desire to be a servant the rest of my life.

Let me share with you another story. A mother was cleaning up the kitchen one evening when her fourteen-year-old son ran through the kitchen into his bedroom. He slammed the door and threw himself on the bed. His mother went into his room to see what was wrong, but he would not talk to her. He just buried his head under the pillow and refused to acknowledge her presence. She sat there quietly for a few minutes, but got no response from her distressed son. So she went back into the kitchen and waited until her husband got home. She was concerned because she had never seen her son this upset.

When her husband arrived, she told him what had happened and how concerned she was. He went to talk with his son. In a gentle, quiet voice, he asked his son how he was doing. No response. His father asked, "Did you go out with your girlfriend tonight?" The son hesitantly said, "Yes." The father asked if the son had done anything wrong. The son answered his father curtly, "No."

A discussion ensued in which they considered whether or not the son and the girlfriend loved each other. As they talked, it became clear that the girl loved the boy more than the boy loved the girl. That was what was bothering him. He did not really care for her, but he realized he was capable of using her for his own enjoyment.

The father was troubled. It is difficult to help children, as they grow, to discover their feelings and attitudes and help them handle those powerful emotions responsibly. So the father and son talked about the difference between using a person for selfish gain and truly giving to a person because you care about him or her.

This dynamic occurs in all kinds of relationships—in business, in politics, between parents and children, and between single people who are attracted to each other. This father told his son that it is often easy to get people to do things for you, even if you don't care for them. For example, it is easy for some people to form friendships with people of importance to reach their goals for success in politics or business. It is easy to get into the habit of finding mutual attraction and using that to fulfill your own wants and desires without caring for the other person.

We discussed the antidote to these vain imaginations earlier; it is choosing to cultivate *storge*. When there is mutual caring, love, and appreciation, we ensure that we are not abusing a relationship. We genuinely care for others, so we look to serve them first. Our godly imaginations should make us realize we are to be caregivers—loving others and serving others, as the Scriptures affirm:

> And let us consider how we may spur one another on toward love and good deeds.
> —HEBREWS 10:24

The essence of satisfaction in life is serving others. If we focus all our energy on ourselves, we will frequently discover many disconcerting and covetous thoughts—anger, envy, lust, and other imaginations that never give us peace. When we think of ourselves rather than others, we are never satisfied, and we seldom find true, purposeful activity. Jesus gave us His example to follow:

> "For even the Son of Man did not come to be served, but
> to serve, and to give his life as a ransom for many."
> —MARK 10:45

Jesus calls Himself the Son of Man about eighty times in the New Testament. This term gives us a rich image of the life of Christ as the representative for all of us. Other terms reveal different aspects of His divine nature. For example, Son of God is a term that reveals Christ's identity as a member of the Trinity: Father, Son, and Holy Spirit.

But as the Son of Man, Jesus served the needs of mankind. The implication, therefore, is that as Jesus served others, so should we. If the Son of Man was a servant, so should all men and women be servants.

And for the follower of Christ, serving is a great delight! It puts our whole being in perspective and provides one of the greatest forms of healthy imaginations. If we are focused on others, we have little time to think of our own needs. We cannot imagine that we are not satisfied when we are involved in trying to satisfy others. The apostle Paul realized this truth when he instructed believers:

> Therefore, as God's chosen people, holy and dearly loved, clothe yourselves with compassion, kindness, humility, gentleness and patience. Bear with each other and forgive whatever grievances you may have against one another. Forgive as the Lord forgave you. And over all these virtues put on love, which binds them all together in perfect unity.
> —COLOSSIANS 3:12–14

In these verses, Paul spells out the imaginations we must have as God's children—imaginations that guide us as we serve others. These are attitudes that will always put others first and help us effectively care for others in our daily life. Not all of us will be professional caregivers, but all of us should care for others because God loves us.

216

Serving others helps us fight selfish imaginations. For example, it is difficult to be proud when we put others first; it is difficult to be filled with anger when we have imaginations of forgiveness; it is difficult to worry when we are filled with imaginations of patience through the Holy Spirit.

We must be able to love others in order to care for them. And we must submit to them so we can care for them. The Scriptures teach:

> Do nothing out of selfish ambition or vain conceit, but in humility consider others better than yourselves.
>
> —PHILIPPIANS 2:3

Caregiving allows us to grow deeper spiritually. When we care for others, we take on their burdens, praying for them and finding practical ways to help. It actually makes us stronger, too. As we serve others, we come closer to God. When we are focused on the Lord as we serve, we glorify Him. We do not act for our own glory.

The apostle Paul offered some practical guidelines for serving, quoted here from Eugene H. Peterson's exciting version of the Bible called *The Message:*

> If you're called to give aid to people in distress, keep your eyes open and be quick to respond; if you work with the disadvantaged, don't let yourself get irritated with them or depressed by them. Keep a smile on your face. Love from the center of who you are; don't fake it. Run for dear life from evil; hold on for dear life to good. Be good friends who love deeply; practice playing second fiddle. Don't burn out; keep yourselves fueled and aflame. Be alert servants of the Master, cheerfully expectant. Don't quit in hard times; pray all the harder. Help needy Christians; be inventive in hospitality.
>
> —ROMANS 12: 8–13, *THE MESSAGE*

Paul offers many principles for serving as well as some warnings. If we try to take on others' burdens and handle them ourselves, we will self-destruct. In all things, we must be servants who are full of God's love, or we will be destroyed.

He describes for us the triangle of service. Christ is the foundation; those who serve and those who are being served are the sides, submitted to each other and to Christ. In marriage, husband and wife are the sides. In an occupation, employer and employee are the sides. We come together to love each other, serve each other, and reach out to others, all the while doing the work of Chirst, who is our foundation.

Whatever we do, no matter how good it is, will not amount to anything unless Jesus is the foundation. Only when we have Jesus permeating our lives will our acts be of value. We need to do His work in His name, by the power of the Holy Spirit living within us.

Our whole life's work is to pursue the Lord's purpose for our life. In all of our imaginations we are to find God's goal and pursue it. We have to ask the Lord to reveal to us His purpose for our lives.

The best attitude we can bring to our vocation or employment is to enjoy it, to believe that it is where we belong, and to see it as our ministry—doing the Lord's work regardless of the task. It has been said that the happiest person you know will be the one who is happiest in his occupation. Most people who are happy in their work are happy with themselves. The two go hand-in-hand.

People who have God's Spirit in their work and in their life demonstrate a spirit of cooperation, harmony, and enjoyment. I believe this was the key difference between two friends of Jesus, sisters named Mary and Martha. Martha was busy working around the house, getting ready for Jesus' visit. On the surface, it seemed like the right attitude to have. She was preparing for the Lord because she loved Him and wanted Him to be comfortable during their time together. But do you remember her attitude when Jesus arrived?

But Martha was distracted by all the preparations that had to be made. She came to him and asked, "Lord, don't you care that my sister has left me to do the work by myself? Tell her to help me!"

—LUKE 10:40

Did Martha find peace in Jesus' presence? Was she happy to be with Him? It doesn't seem that way. She appeared to be more concerned about how much she was doing. Even more, she was concerned about how little her sister was doing. She was proud of her accomplishments and critical of her sister. And she wanted Jesus to side with her and tell Mary to get moving.

How would you respond to Martha's complaint? Jesus said:

"Martha, Martha," the Lord answered, "you are worried and upset about many things, but only one thing is needed. Mary has chosen what is better, and it will not be taken away from her."

—LUKE 10:41–42

Actions matter less than attitude. It was important that Martha prepared the house and cared for the guests. But more important was her attitude. While Martha was scurrying around, Mary was sitting at Jesus' feet, listening to Him. Martha was "distracted by the preparations." Mary was focused on Jesus and looked to Him.

It is the same with us. Jesus sees through our work to the inner attitude that directs our actions. He knows when the Holy Spirit is guiding us and when our own desire for praise or success is directing us. Our work must be guided by God's Spirit, rather than our own goals. When we try to work under our own power, we are focused on worldly standards of success. As a result, we become tense in our work, creating an attitude of burnout that can destroy our health.

There is a satisfying kind of tiredness when we have put in a productive day's work. We feel we have been useful. But if we try to do too much or carry that feeling too far, then we become

219

exhausted. I constantly ask the Lord to teach me not to do any work for my own goals. My strength is renewed when I am resting in my relationship with Him, sensing His guidance. I know I cannot do His work solely through my efforts. He must lead me. His strength supports me. The Scriptures instruct us:

> Let us not become weary in doing good, for at the proper time we will reap a harvest if we do not give up.
> —GALATIANS 6:9

When we do our work with the Spirit of the Lord guiding us, the life of Jesus blossoms within us. We have His joy, His peace, His eternal vision leading us. When we live in His energy and His power, we have great peace and great activity. We have His equipping power guiding us in our work, allowing us to act without the distractions of this world. We can focus on our work through Him, with His ease and patience, and we experience joy in it.

It is possible to think we are doing what God wants us to do, yet still miss the mark. The test is whether we are enjoying the work or whether we are anxious and worried about the work. Do we do the best we can and not worry about the rest? When we call ourselves Christian and work to do what Christ guides us to do, we must let Him take charge. We must abide in His presence.

Do we ask Jesus to be in our business and career decisions? As we buy and sell, do we ask Jesus if that is what He would have us do? Is it greed or godly thinking that motivates our choices?

Many people in the workplace tend to think they have to worry about the attitude of others around them, their working conditions, and other external circumstances. Certainly these factors have an influence on our ability to perform our job. But more essential is how we focus our minds at work and what we allow ourselves to be concerned with.

We need to make wise decisions for Jesus—decisions that honor and glorify Him. May our decisions show we have truly been crucified and that Christ lives in us.

CHAPTER 29

A Mind of Faith

God is so great we cannot fully comprehend Him. And we understand very little about earth, let alone heaven. So how do we think we can truly take on the mind of Christ? How can we unite our minds with His?

Our faith in God's grace enables us to enter into a deeply personal and intimate relationship with Him. With imaginations of faith we enter God's mind of grace and we are in union with Him.

God's grace is revealed in the faith of believers in the Old Testament and the New Testament. For example, God's grace was at work in the life of Abraham, who believed he could have a child at age one hundred; who believed he could go out in faith from his people and form a new group of people to be God's people; who believed those people would cover the earth. Let's consider a few truths that the Bible teaches us about God, about faith, and about our relationship with our Creator, Redeemer, and Sustainer:

> Great is the LORD and most worthy of praise; his greatness no one can fathom.
>
> —PSALM 145:3

Earlier we discussed the complexity of a single cell. There is an irreducible complexity in the single cell that cannot be understood in spite of all the advances in medical science. By simple definition, a cell is a very small unit of protoplasm, usually with a nucleus and an enclosing membrane. All plants and animals are made up of one or more cells. Yet, no one understands all the mechanisms of a single cell or how to make one.

As I mentioned earlier, when I studied the cell's complexities as a medical student, I understood that there was a Creator, and I experienced my own personal "quickening." All doubt was gone regarding the existence of God as I saw physical evidence that could not have occurred by chance or evolution, but had to have been intelligently designed.

I realized that the mind which had designed that one single cell—so simple yet so complex—was greater than any human mind could even begin to understand.

There is an irreducible complexity in the stars and the stratosphere that truly cannot be understood by man, let alone designed by him. Astronomers now realize that the universe has more than a dozen evenly distributed clumps of galaxies. One of the clumps of galaxies closest to the earth measures 500 million light years long, 200 million light years wide, and 15 million light years thick. In case your high school astronomy has grown fuzzy, a light year is a little less than 6 trillion miles! And God, our Creator, calls the stars by name (Psalm 147:4) while He listens to our heart's cry! What a God He is! Listen to the psalmist:

> Praise the LORD. How good it is to sing praises to our God, how pleasant and fitting to praise him! The LORD builds up Jerusalem; he gathers the exiles of Israel. He heals the brokenhearted and binds up their wounds. He determines the number of the stars and calls them each by name. Great is our Lord and mighty in power; his understanding has no limit.
>
> —PSALM 147:1–5

God's understanding is without limit; it is infinite! The word *infinite* means to extend beyond measure or comprehension, endless, immense, inexhaustible. This psalm tells us that God's understanding is as vast as the stars that He calls by name, but as intimate as knowing each person's innermost needs.

There is an irreducible complexity in the integration of both the small and large in everything we see. Even the greatest minds in physics cannot explain how all the physical laws integrate together in the beautiful manner that is absolutely required for the coordination of the universe and for life to exist.

This irreducible complexity of both the small and the large, and the integration in between, tells us there must be some person, some mind, which was in the beginning who had the knowledge to create everything—because He knew everything.

In today's world of technology, we have achieved incredible feats. Our inventions are awesome. But with all our ingenuity, we still cannot create something from nothing. Only God can do that!

The mind of God is to be worshiped and reckoned with in our lives as we understand that we are not the wisdom of the age—rather, we are the product of the wisdom of He who created the ages! As Job understood:

> God's voice thunders in marvelous ways; he does great
> things beyond our understanding.
>
> —JOB 37:5

It takes a wise person to look at the complexity of a single cell or of the entire universe and realize there must be a God. Faith does not abandon natural reasoning. Faith says, "There is a scientific relationship to God that exists with what we cannot see."

> By faith we understand that the universe was formed at
> God's command, so that what is seen was not made out
> of what was visible.
>
> —HEBREWS 11:3

Faith cannot be explained by natural laws. We can understand those laws, but we also realize we cannot explain life or eternity. In the irreducible complexity of all life forms we acknowledge God's awesome power—power that is beyond what we see, what we understand, what we comprehend.

Consider the happy marriage relationship between a husband and wife. While the partners do not always understand each other, they trust each other. And their faith and trust brings about true intimacy.

It is similar in our relationship with God. We may not understand God fully, but we trust Him, we have faith in Him. Our hope is in Him, resulting in a satisfying relationship with Him. The Scriptures describe faith for us:

> Now faith is being sure of what we hope for and certain of what we do not see.
>
> —HEBREWS 11:1

> We live by faith, not by sight.
>
> —2 CORINTHIANS 5:7

This is the essence of faith—believing beyond what we see and understand and trusting in God, the Creator of all. Now, we can look at the universe and marvel at the power of God. We can believe in that power. But our faith is not activated until we believe in another aspect of God's power: the power of the resurrection. Accepting the reality of the resurrection of Christ activates our faith in God. God is so powerful, not even death could stop Him!

There is a reason for this amazing demonstration of divine power. It is the greatest expression of love in the universe: the agreement of the Father and the Son for Christ to be sacrificed on the cross as an atonement for our sin:

> For God so loved the world that he gave his one and only Son, that whoever believes in him shall not perish but have eternal life.
>
> —JOHN 3:16

He died on the cross so that every sinner who trusts in Him will find complete forgiveness for all their sins. That was His purpose for coming to earth as a man:

> Here is a trustworthy saying that deserves full accep-
> tance: Christ Jesus came into the world to save sinners.
> —1 TIMOTHY 1:15

According to the Scriptures, through His death and resurrection, we receive eternal life!

> "I am the resurrection and the life. He who believes in
> me will live, even though he dies; and whoever lives
> and believes in me will never die."
> —JOHN 11:25–26

> "I tell you the truth, he who believes has everlasting
> life."
> —JOHN 6:47

This is the matchless grace of God! This is God's pure and
perfect grace—His mind for mankind. The climax of God's
grace is seen on the cross, when Jesus took all our sins upon
Himself and said, "It is finished." His merciful redemption—
His grace—saves us from the power of sin:

> For it is by grace you have been saved, through faith—
> and this not from yourselves, it is the gift of God—not
> by works, so that no one can boast.
> —EPHESIANS 2:8–9

What is our response to such an overwhelming gift of love
and grace? Should we be arrogant, thinking we don't need
grace? No! All of us are sinners in need of this grace. We must
deny our self-righteous imaginations and choose to live the life
of faith. There is nothing more basic to the Christian life than
a conscious sense of our daily need of Christ.

We cannot earn God's grace, for we all are sinners. Instead,
we must believe in a God who is merciful and who has love,
grace, and mercy for those who are in Him. Our only response

should be to accept this gift of redemption—to surrender ourselves to God and to be born again by God's grace and by His Spirit, as the Scriptures teach:

> Jesus answered, "I tell you the truth, no one can enter the kingdom of God unless he is born of water and the Spirit."
> —JOHN 3:5

Faith goes beyond the power we see exhibited in creation. Faith is an unconditional commitment to our Lord that brings our minds to His mind. Faith is a relationship with God—a relationship that begins when we believe in Him and draw near to Him:

> Come near to God and he will come near to you.
> —JAMES 4:8

To draw near means to be aligned to God—being satisfied with Him and enjoying Him. These attitudes of affection strengthen our relationship with God. We are engulfed and intertwined with Him. Ours is a dynamic and dramatic relationship!

> May [Christ] dwell in you hearts through faith. And I pray that you, being rooted and established in love, may have power, together with all the saints, to grasp how wide and long and high and deep is the love of Christ, and to know this love that surpasses knowledge—that you may be filled to the measure of all the fullness of God.
> —EPHESIANS 3:17-19

This is the God who created a single cell and the vast universe! This is the Almighty, who loves us so much He let His Son die on the cross! As we accept this truth, we are filled with faith in the unseen fullness of God. We experience His eternal love and eternal life. We experience *metanoia* (changed thoughts) through our unconditional faith in His grace when we are born again as the children of God!

> Therefore, if anyone is in Christ, he is a new creation; the
> old has gone, the new has come!
> —2 CORINTHIANS 5:17

We are God's created people. When we look to Him with a mind-set of faith, we are engulfed and intimately entwined with His mind of grace. We cannot comprehend His wisdom, but we can believe His promises:

> And this is what he has promised us—even eternal life.
> —1 JOHN 2:25

The promises of God change people, and change people's minds, so they can be at one with God's mind of grace, as the apostle Paul declared:

> But by the grace of God I am what I am, and his grace to
> me was not without effect. No, I worked harder than all of
> them—yet, not I, but the grace of God that was with me.
> —1 CORINTHIANS 15:10

To avoid becoming spiritual "couch potatoes," as we discussed, we must live out our faith in God's mind of grace. For example, we have been forgiven by God. Therefore, we must forgive others. Our purpose in life is the opposite of becoming a "couch potato." Our purpose is to live out our transforming faith in His grace. Our mind-set and our actions will tell us when we are on the right track—when we find true satisfaction in Him.

We glorify God most by being aligned with His mind of grace, being satisfied with Him, having faith in Him, and enjoying Him. We find true contentment in Him. We find a sense of love, of well-being, of delight, of hope, and of anticipation. We have no desire for anything other than Christ!

We live our lives before an audience of one—our Lord and Savior, Jesus Christ. We are totally satisfied in Jesus, with no wants for what this world offers. We are sublimely at peace with

God. What He has, whatever He gives, satisfies us. All we do is ask every day what God wants, and then do what God wants.

Our sense of satisfaction glorifies God. We enhance God's glory when the way we live calls attention to His majesty. We do not make God better; we simply make His greatness more apparent to others. To display the glory of God should be our purpose in everything.

> "This is to my Father's glory, that you bear much fruit, showing yourselves to be my disciples."
> —JOHN 15:8

We integrate eternity into our life every day when our sense of satisfaction glorifies God. He is our portion, and we are filled with peace, joy, thanksgiving, and love.

This is the true effect of our thoughts on our lives. How we think now affects our present life and our eternity! There is so much to live for in godly imaginations.

Conclusion

Why are our imaginations so important? Do we establish our hope in God so that we have joy and power? Do we live out the commandments of God so that we are sanctified? Do we have peace because we believe in His future grace? Do we have power because we allow the Holy Spirit to direct our lives instead of trying to be in charge ourselves? Do we allow all of these dynamics to change our life?

These mental attitudes are very important for a changed life. We must enact in life what we know to be correct: the Word of God in our minds, as seen in the person of Jesus Christ. Listen to this advice from the apostle Paul:

> Do not be deceived: God cannot be mocked. A man reaps what he sows. The one who sows to please his sinful nature, from that nature will reap destruction; the one who sows to please the Spirit, from the Spirit will reap eternal life.
>
> —GALATIANS 6:7–8

Our fate for eternity hangs in the balance. If we have godly thoughts, we reap godly blessings now and always. If we have earthly thoughts, we reap an unfulfilled life full of the sins that stem from selfishness. Our sinful nature, left unchecked, will destroy us. We will never find perfect peace, joy, and love through the imaginations of this world.

Let's review the rich blessings of focusing our imaginations on the Lord. The moment we surrender to Christ, we are engulfed and empowered by the Holy Spirit. We are translated from the temporal to the eternal. We reap everlasting life with the Creator of the universe. What greater harvest can there be?

Our present thoughts are the building blocks that determine how we live in eternity. Are we surrendered to Christ? Then we seek Him every day. Are we focused more on the diversions of this world, the fleeting pleasures that money and success can buy? Then we will spend eternity without Him.

Let me tell you about a friend of mine, Jamie Buckingham. At first, Jamie had trouble accepting the reality of his diagnosis of cancer. For a year and a half, through tests and operations and various medical procedures, Jamie kept asking God what he was supposed to learn from all this. Jamie waged a valiant battle against cancer and enjoyed a series of miracles against the disease. And then he died.

But before he died, Jamie understood. He knew the Lord was saying it was time for the two of them to get closer. Jamie was released from the fear of death because he walked closer than ever to the Lord. He told how he was no longer concerned with the church he pastored, his writings, and other priorities that had previously been so important to him. He was completely attuned to God's presence because he was stripped of the worldly concerns of this life. There no longer was all the clutter of daily life, the obligations, activities, and agendas of the world. It was just Jamie and Jesus; Jesus and Jamie.

He was living the New Testament reality of eternal life:

> Therefore we do not lose heart. Though outwardly we are wasting away, yet inwardly we are being renewed day by day. For our light and momentary troubles are achieving for us an eternal glory that far outweighs them all. So we fix our eyes not on what is seen, but on what is unseen. For what is seen is temporary, but what is unseen is eternal.
> —2 CORINTHIANS 4:16–18

God wants us to be spiritually one with Him, appreciating that He created us and that He desires to be one with us for eternity in our minds and in our existence. Our life's purpose is to live with Him and not by ourselves. Our union with Him involves His perfect plan for our lives. The Lord God is with us and in us throughout the day. We never tire of beholding His great, irreducible complexity in creation. We stand in awe of His love, His great beauty, and His great saving grace through His Son who gave up everything for us!

This is the reason we live! Those who find this purpose for living find the richest of all blessings now and forever—Him.

God says to His children, in essence: I will be with you all the time. I will make sure every minute of life is filled with what is best for you, the most interesting for you, the most rewarding for you, and that you will leave this earth to enter eternity knowing you chose the absolute best.

We have to be with Him by knowing Him, becoming like Him, serving Him, and being in eternity with Him. At the end of our life, we will be judged not for what we did, but whether we did it within the context of a relationship with Christ—whether we did it with His love, His peace, and with imaginations of Him.

This exclusive imagination of being with Him requires a great deal of focus that is strengthened through Bible study, prayer, and relationships with other believers. Any time we let worldly imaginations enter in, we become vulnerable to drifting away from Him. We can lose the purpose of life by becoming preoccupied with imaginations of the world rather than imaginations of God.

Our challenge in life is to see whether we can be totally sold out to Christ. And our attitude today determines our attitude for eternity. We need to seek that goal of completely honoring Him daily. We need to give ourselves to Him cheerfully and joyfully. We need to give our work to Him. We need to give our money to Him. We need to give our all to Him.

The Westminster Catechism says, "The chief end of man is to glorify God and enjoy Him forever." God wants us to glorify Him and enjoy Him forever. He wants us to be totally focused on Him. We must have a mind-set of glorifying our Eternal Partner forever.

We glorify Him by worshiping Him. That worship starts at the cross, where we bow and receive His forgiveness for our sins from the risen Lord Jesus. We surrender ourselves to Him. Then we can enjoy the person of Christ, our Creator, now and forever. Nothing separates us from Him.

Author John Piper says this in a slightly different way. He writes, in his book, *Future Grace*, "The chief end of man is to glorify God by enjoying Him forever."[1] This is the essence of imaginations that are filled with eternal faith in the grace of our Lord. We begin to understand the wonder of our position in Christ:

> Since, then, you have been raised with Christ, set your hearts on things above, where Christ is seated at the right hand of God. Set your minds on things above, not on earthly things. For you died, and your life is now hidden with Christ in God. When Christ, who is your life, appears, then you also will appear with him in glory.
>
> —Colossians 3:1–4

Our ultimate imagination is to glorify God by enjoying Him! There is nothing other than the person of Jesus, because in the person of Jesus all things are centered, and around Him all things revolve. He is our portion in life. He is our eternity. He will do far more than we can think and comprehend—exceedingly and abundantly so! (Ephesians 3:20). His power will work in us to bring glory to God through us—His people, the church. He is the most wonderful imagination of the mind! Amen and amen!

Epilogue

When you wake up in the morning, do you wake up happy? Do you wake up with joy in your heart, wanting to live this day with enthusiasm? Do you wake up with thanksgiving and love? The attitude you have every morning determines the attitude you will have for eternity. I encourage you to review the three basic principles of *Imaginations*:

1. We are what we think; therefore, our thoughts determine our actions.

We have imaginations, which form thoughts, actions, habits, and character. We really become who we are as a result of our thoughts.

2. Our present thoughts affect how we will spend eternity.

When our thoughts are faithfully focused on God, we will be rewarded in eternity. We have an initial glimpse of eternity now, and we will be richly rewarded in His presence in heaven.

3. God is most glorified in us when we are most satisfied in Him.

We must truly surrender to the satisfaction of being with Jesus and letting Him provide for us. This mind-set frees us from daily worry and concern. Our relationship with Him is the foundation for all our thoughts and actions. It replaces negative attitudes with positive imaginations based on Christ, filling us with peace, joy, and love. And it allows us to be effective in our work for Him.

Scripture Index

Notes

CHAPTER 1
WE ARE WHAT WE THINK

1. Quoted at Motivational and Inspirational Quotes, 2002-2003, found at www.motivational-inspirational-corner.com /getquote.html(accessed May 28, 2004).

2. *Biblesoft's New Exhaustive Strong's Numbers and Concordance with Expanded Greek-Hebrew Dictionary.* Copyright © 1994, Biblesoft and International Bible Translators, Inc., s.v. *yetser*, Strong's number 3336.

3. Ibid., s.v. *hagah*, Strong's number 1897

4. Ibid., s.v. *dialogismos*, Strong's number 1261, translated *imagination, reasoning, thought.*

CHAPTER 2
SEARCHING FOR SATISFACTION

1. John Piper, *Future Grace* (Sisters, OR: Multnomah Books, 1995), 9.

2. *The New Strong's Expanded Exhaustive Concordance of the Bible.* (Nashville, TN: Thomas Nelson Publishers, 2001) s.v. *mentonia*, Strong's number 3341.

CHAPTER 6
CHANGED HEARTS, CHANGED LIVES

1. Quoted in Nigel Clifford, *Christian Preachers* (Bryntirion, Wales: Evangelical Press of Wales, 1994), 152.

CHAPTER 8
A NEW PERSPECTIVE

1. Quoted at WSN Press, Campus Crusade for Christ, 1994, found at www.campuscrusadeforchrist.com/resources /interactive/LiveItUp (accessed June 7, 2004).

2. John Piper, *Future Grace* (Sisters, OR: Multnomah Books, 1995).

CHAPTER 9
THE MOTIVATION EQUATION

1. William Standish Reed, *Surgery of the Soul. Healing the Whole Person—Spirit, Mind and Body* (Tampa, FL: Christian Medical Foundation International, 1995).

CHAPTER II
COMMUNION WITH CHRIST

1. *Biblesoft's New Exhaustive Strong's Numbers and Concordance with Expanded Greek-Hebrew Dictionary.* Copyright © 1994, Biblesoft and International Bible Translators, Inc., s.v. *tsaba*, Strong's number 6633.

CHAPTER 17
MAKING OUR CHOICE

1. Richard Baxter, *The Saints' Everlasting Rest* (Fearn, U.K.: Christian Focus Publications, 1998).

CHAPTER 18
SPIRITUAL CONDITIONING

1. *Biblesoft's New Exhaustive Strong's Numbers and Concordance with Expanded Greek-Hebrew Dictionary.* Copyright © 1994, Biblesoft and International Bible Translators, Inc., s.v. *deesis*, Strong's number 1189.

CHAPTER 21
LETTING OUR LIGHT SHINE

1. Clebe McClary and Diane Barker, *Living Proof* (Clebe McClary Evangelistic Association, 1978).

CHAPTER 22
ABANDONED TO GOD

1. William Lane Craig, "The Teleological Argument and the Anthropic Principle," September 27, 2003, found at www.leaderu.com/offices/billcraig/docs/teleo.html (accessed May 20, 2004).

CHAPTER 24
THE STRONG FOUNDATION

1. C. S. Lewis, *The Four Loves* (San Diego, CA: Harcourt Brace & Co., 1988), 31.

CHAPTER 28
A LIFE OF CARING

1. Eugene H. Peterson, *The Message: The New Testament in Contemporary Language* (Colorado Springs, CO: Navpress, 1993).

CONCLUSION

1. John Piper, *Future Grace* (Sisters, OR: Multnomah Books, 1995), 398.

About the Author

James P. Gills, M.D., received his medical degree from Duke University Medical Center in 1959. He served his ophthalmology residency at Wilmer Ophthalmological Institute of Johns Hopkins University from 1962–1965. Dr. Gills founded the St. Luke's Cataract and Laser Institute in Tarpon Springs, Florida, and has performed more cataract and lens implant surgeries than any other eye surgeon in the world. Since establishing his Florida practice in 1968, he has been firmly committed to embracing new technology and perfecting the latest cataract surgery techniques. In 1974, he became the first eye surgeon in the U.S. to dedicate his practice to cataract treatment through the use of intraocular lenses. Dr. Gills has been recognized in Florida and throughout the world for his professional accomplishments and personal commitment to helping others. He has been recognized by the readers of *Cataract & Refractive Surgery Today* as one of the top 50 cataract and refractive opinion leaders.

As a world-renowned ophthalmologist, Dr. Gills has received innumerable medical and educational awards. In 2005, he was especially honored to receive the Duke Medical Alumni Association's Humanitarian Award. In 2007, he was blessed with a particularly treasured double honor. Dr. Gills was elected to the Johns Hopkins Society of Scholars and was also selected to receive the Distinguished Medical Alumnus Award, the highest honor bestowed by Johns Hopkins School of Medicine. Dr. Gills thereby became the first physician in the country to receive high honors twice in two weeks from the prestigious Johns Hopkins University in Baltimore.

In the years 1994 through 2004, Dr. Gills was listed in *The Best Doctors in America*. As a clinical professor of ophthalmology at the University of South Florida, he was named one of the best Ophthalmologists in America in 1996 by ophthalmic academic leaders nationwide. He has served on the Board of Directors of the American College of Eye Surgeons, the Board of Visitors at Duke University Medical Center, and the Advisory Board of Wilmer Ophthalmological Institute at Johns Hopkins University. Listed in Marquis' *Who's Who in America*, Dr. Gills was Entrepreneur of the Year 1990 for the State of Florida, received the Tampa Bay Business Hall of Fame Award in 1993, and was given the Tampa Bay Ethics Award from the University of Tampa in 1995. In 1996, he was awarded the prestigious Innovators Award by his colleagues in the American Society of Cataract and Refractive Surgeons. In 2000, he was named Philanthropist of the Year by the National Society of Fundraising Executives, was presented with the Florida Enterprise Medal by the Merchants Association of Florida, was named Humanitarian of the Year by the Golda Meir/Kent Jewish Center in Clearwater, and was honored as Free Enterpriser of the Year by the Florida Council on Economic Education. In 2001, The Salvation Army presented Dr. Gills their prestigious "Others Award" in honor of his lifelong commitment to service and caring.

Virginia Polytechnic Institute, Dr. Gills' alma mater, presented their University Distinguished Achievement Award to him in 2003. In that same year, Dr. Gills was appointed by Governor Jeb Bush to the Board of Directors of the Florida Sports Foundation. In 2004, Dr. Gills was invited to join the prestigious Florida Council of 100, an advisory committee reporting directly to the governor on various aspects of Florida's public policy affecting the quality of life and the economic well-being of all Floridians.

While Dr. Gills has many accomplishments and varied interests, his primary focus is to restore physical vision to patients and to bring spiritual enlightenment through his life. Guided by his strong and enduring faith in Jesus Christ, he seeks to encourage and comfort the patients who come to St. Luke's and to share his faith whenever possible. It was through sharing his insights with patients that he initially began writing on Christian topics. An avid student of the Bible for many years, he now has authored nineteen books on Christian living, with over eight million copies in print. With the exception of the Bible, Dr. Gills' books are the most widely requested books in the U.S. prison system. They have been supplied to over two thousand prisons and jails, including every death row facility in the nation. In addition, Dr. Gills has published more than 195 medical articles and has authored or coauthored ten medical reference textbooks. Six of those books were bestsellers at the American Academy of Ophthalmology annual meetings.

As an ultra-distance athlete, Dr. Gills participated in forty-six marathons, including eighteen Boston marathons and fourteen 100-mile mountain runs. In addition, he completed five Ironman Triathlons in Hawaii and holds the record for completing six Double Ironman Triathlons, each within the thirty-six hour maximum time frame. Dr. Gills has served on the National Board of Directors of the Fellowship of Christian Athletes and, in 1991, was the first recipient of their Tom Landry Award. A passionate athlete, surgeon, and scientist, Dr. Gills is also a member of the Explorers Club, a prestigious, multi-disciplinary society dedicated to advancing field research, scientific exploration, and the ideal that it is vital to preserve the instinct to explore.

Married in 1962, Dr. Gills and his wife, Heather, have raised two children, Shea and Pit. Shea Gills Grundy, a former attorney and now full-time mom, is a graduate of Vanderbilt University and Emory Law School. She and her husband, Shane Grundy, M.D., have four children: twins Maggie and Braddock, Jimmy, and Lily Grace. The Gills' son, J. Pit Gills, M.D., ophthalmologist, received his medical degree from Duke University Medical Center and, in 2001, joined the St. Luke's practice. "Dr. Pit" and his wife, Joy, have three children: Pitzer, Parker, and Stokes.

The Writings of James P. Gills, M.D.

A Biblical Economics Manifesto
(With Ron H. Nash, Ph.D.)
The best understanding of economics aligns with what the Bible teaches on the subject.
ISBN: 978-0-88419-871-0
E-book ISBN: 978-1-59979-925-4

Believe and Rejoice: Changed by Faith, Filled With Joy
Observe how faith in God can let us see His heart of joy.
ISBN: 978-1-59979-169-2
E-book ISBN: 978-1-61638-727-3

Come Unto Me: God's Call to Intimacy
Inspired by Dr. Gills' trip to Mt. Sinai, this book explores God's eternal desire for mankind to know Him intimately.
ISBN: 978-1-59185-214-8
E-book ISBN: 978-1-61638-728-0

Darwinism Under the Microscope: How Recent Scientific Evidence Points to Divine Design
(With Tom Woodward, PhD)
Behold the wonder of it all! The facts glorify our Intelligent Creator!
ISBN: 978-0-88419-925-0
E-book ISBN: 978-1-59979-882-0

The Dynamics of Worship
Designed to rekindle a passionate love for God, this book gives who, what, where, when, why, and how of worship
ISBN: 978-1-59185-657-3
E-book ISBN: 978-1-61638-725-9

Exceeding Gratitude for the Creator's Plan: Discover the Life-Changing Dynamic of Appreciation
Standing in awe of the creation and being secure in the knowledge of our heavenly hope, the thankful believer abounds in appreciation for the Creator's wondrous plan.
(Hardcover) ISBN: 978-1-59979-162-3/ 978-1-59979-155-5
E-book ISBN: 978-1-61638-729-7

God's Prescription for Healing: Five Divine Gifts of Healing
Explore the wonders of healing by design, now and forevermore.
ISBN: 978-1-59185-286-5
(Hardcover) ISBN: 978-0-88419-947-2
E-book ISBN: 978-1-61638-730-3

Imaginations: More Than You Think
Focusing our thoughts will help us grow closer to God.
ISBN: 978-1-59185-609-2
E-book ISBN: 978-1-59979-883-7

Love: Fulfilling the Ultimate Quest
Enjoy a quick refresher course on the meaning and method of God's great gift.
ISBN: 978-1-59979-235-4
E-book ISBN: 978-1-61638-731-7

Overcoming Spiritual Blindness
Jesus + anything = nothing. Jesus + nothing = everything. Here is a book that will help you recognize the many facets of spiritual blindness as you seek to fulfill the Lord's plan for your life.
ISBN: 978-1-59185-607-8
E-book ISBN: 978-1-59979-884-4

Rx for Worry: A Thankful Heart
Trust your future to the God who is in eternal control.
ISBN: 978-1-59979-090-9
E-book ISBN: 978-1-59979-926-1

The Prayerful Spirit: Passion for God, Compassion for People
Dr. Gills tells how prayer has changed his life as well as the lives of patients and other doctors. It will change your life also!
ISBN: 978-1-59185-215-5
E-book ISBN: 978-1-61638-732-7

The Unseen Essential: A Story for Our Troubled Times...
Part One
This compelling, contemporary novel portrays one man's transformation through the power of God's love.
ISBN: 978-1-59185-810-2
E-book ISBN: 978-1-59979-513-3

Tender Journey: A Story for Our Troubled Times...
Part Two
Be enriched by the popular sequel to *The Unseen Essential*.
ISBN: 978-1-59185-809-6
E-book ISBN: 978-1-59979-509-6

DID YOU ENJOY THIS BOOK?

We at Love Press would be pleased to hear from you if
Imaginations: More Than You Think
has had an effect in your life or the lives of your loved ones.
Send your letters to:

Love Press
P.O. Box 5000
Tarpon Springs, FL 34688-5000